Who is the Holy Spirit?

Charles Massabki O.S.B.

Translated by John Auricchio

ALBA · HOUSE   NEW · YORK

SOCIETY OF ST. PAUL, 2187 VICTORY BLVD., STATEN ISLAND, NEW YORK 10314

Library of Congress Cataloging in Publication Data

Massabki, Charles.
    Who is the Holy Spirit?

    Translation of Qui est l'esprit saint?
    1. Holy Spirit. I. Title.
BT121.1M3213   231'.3   79-15184
ISBN: 0-8189-0390-2

Nihil Obstat:
Daniel V. Flynn, J.C.D.
Censor Librorum

Imprimatur:
Joseph T. O'Keefe, Vicar General
Archdiocese of New York
June 1, 1979

The Nihil Obstat and Imprimatur are
a declaration that a book or pamphlet is considered
to be free from doctrinal or moral error. It is not implied
that those who have granted the Nihil Obstat and
Imprimatur agree with the contents,
opinions or statements expressed.

Designed, printed and bound in the United States of
America by the Fathers and Brothers of the
Society of St. Paul, 2187 Victory Boulevard,
Staten Island, New York, 10314, as part of their
communications apostolate.

---

1 2 3 4 5 6 7 8 9 (Current Printing: first digit).

Contents

Preface

To the question posed by me, in the title of this book, *Who is the Holy Spirit*, the answer that I have given is far from having exhausted the subject. Nevertheless, though the Holy Spirit has revealed himself as a Person without a visage, probably because he is love, this study permits us to conjecture, at least, the most outstanding traits of his personality.

In conclusion, I may summarize that the Holy Spirit is the Breath of Love of the Father and the Son, through whom they communicate their love to each other, in the ecstasy of an unending joy.

Because he is Love:

the Holy Spirit is the Life-Giver, who in the beginning, hovered over primordial waters, and through whom all beings receive life;

the Holy Spirit is the Enlightener, under whose inspiration and power, the Prophets and the righteous men of God of the Old Covenant, spoke, acted and gave witness to the Word of the Lord, as he revealed progressively his design of grace and love;

the Holy Spirit is the Regenerator, the power of the Most High, who covered with his shadow the Virgin Mary that she might become the Mother of the Son of God; and who prepared her to be a worthy dwelling place for him;

the Holy Spirit is the Consecrator, through whose action Jesus grew up in wisdom and grace, and who descended upon him on the day of his baptism, that he might be anointed with power to announce the Word of God and to establish his reign, through the Cross;

the Holy Spirit is the Advocate, who descended upon

the Apostles, on the day of Pentecost, and who spoke through them when they gave witness to Christ and to his Resurrection and Ascension.

Because he is the Love of the Father and the Son:

the Holy Spirit is the paternal Love, by whom we have been engendered sons of God, in his only Son, making of us gods and living temples of the Holy Trinity.

the Holy Spirit is the filial Love, who makes us cry: Abba, *Beloved Father!*

Because he is Love:

the Holy Spirit is the Intercessor, who pleads within us with unutterable groanings;

the Holy Spirit is the Unifier, who gathers together all mankind in the unique Body of Christ, making of men brothers, and who builds the Church by pouring upon her his gifts and charisms;

the Holy Spirit is the Quickener, who animates the Church, and by whom her members are directed, taught and sanctified;

the Holy Spirit is the Iconograph, who imprints in each of us the image of Christ, to make us similar to him.

Because he is Love, the Holy Spirit is the Gift of the Father and of the Son, in whom the Love of God is outpoured in our hearts in abundance "for the praise of his glory" (Ep 1:6).

Who is the Holy Spirit?

CHAPTER ONE

The Unrecognized God

The Holy Spirit is the least known Person of the Holy Trinity. A bishop has recently entitled a book on the Holy Spirit, *The Unappreciated Divine Person.* He is unrecognized or unappreciated because he is inadequately known, not to say almost unknown, by too many Christians. In 1897, Pope Leo XIII wrote: "Today there are perhaps Christians who were they to be asked, as St. Paul asked some converts at Ephesus, whether they received the Holy Spirit, would answer like them: 'We have not even heard that there is a Holy Spirit!' " (Encyclical, *Divinum illud munus*) The Pope's words are still actual in our days.

The Holy Spirit who is the soul of the Church, her principle of activity, strength and life; who moves, inspires and directs her; who dwells in us through sanctifying grace, remains the Great Unappreciated God, by numerous Christians, whether nominal or practicing. To be sure, the Sacrament of Confirmation held their attention for a moment, and led them to reflect a little on the Third Person of the Holy Trinity, but they did not attach a great importance to this sacrament. Indeed, Confirmation leaves with people less memories than does their first Communion. Most people know little about the seven gifts of the Spirit and even less the meaning and value of charisms.

The failure to recognize or appreciate the Holy Spirit and his role in the Church and in Christians, produces baneful effects on the practice of the Christian religion, reducing it to a moralistic, legalistic and formalist affair.

Moralistic. The Christian religion lived without the dynamic action of the Holy Spirit of Love, finds itself reduced mostly, if not completely, to a struggle more or less sustained to acquire a certain conduct of life according to an ideal of perfection, more or less high; an ideal which one seeks to attain by the exertions of one's own will, and which rarely successfully risks to engender weariness and discouragement. Religion ceases then to be a living faith in a God who is Love and who loves men to the point of giving them his Son to make *gods* of them, by making them "partakers of the divine nature," as St. Peter writes, and by making them live of his very Life. Indeed, to be aware that we are loved by God as sons, as his own Son and with the same love; to be aware that we are called to enter, beginning with our terrestrial life, in his intimate Trinitarian life—all this is a totally different thing than to reduce the Christian religion to a mere practice of the moral virtues.

Legalistic. Lived without the dynamic action of the Holy Spirit, secondly, the Christian religion becomes a legalistic affair. The commandments risk then to be observed in an exterior and literal fashion, for fear of punishments, and not because evil is evil. Instead of obeying them from the impulse of love, one will refrain from doing, for fear of the sanctions of the law, what one will continue to desire. Not vivified by love, the commandments, not freed from the letter that kills, become an annoying code of unmixed prohibitions which torment; constraints imposed in tiresome and withering forms of repression. Thus they invariably cause guilt complexes, which depress and engender fear, sadness and anguish.

Formalistic. Lived without the dynamic action of the Holy Spirit, thirdly, the Christian falls into formalism. Religious life, i.e., the expression of our relationship with God, otherwise called the life of prayer, becomes the recitation of a set of routine formulas, uttered mechanically, more as a matter of conscience than expression of faith vivified by the breath of love,, which should animate the relations of children of God with their Father, or of disciples of Christ with their Lord, Savior and Friend. Religion then becomes a purely ritualistic affair. It becomes an exterior practice, a rite devoid of spirit. Deprived of the breath of love, the Mass itself risks ceasing to be the worship in spirit and truth, the kind of worship God expects of Christians. Then the Mass becomes an exterior practice, a rite without a soul, and Christians merit the same reproaches that God addressed to the Hebrews in the Old Testament:

What care I for the number of your sacrifices? says the Lord. I have had enough of whole-burnt rams and fat of fatlings; in the blood of calves, lambs and goats I find no pleasure.

When you come to visit me, who asks these things of you? Trample my courts no more! Bring no more worthless offering; your incense is loathsome to me. New moon and sabbath, calling of assemblies, octaves with wickedness: these I cannot bear. Your new moons and festivals I detest; they weigh me down, I tire of the load. When you spread out your hands, I close my eyes to you; though you pray the more, I will not listen. Your hands are full of blood! Put away your misdeeds from before my eyes; cease doing evil; learn to do good. Make justice your aim; redress the wronged, hear the orphan's plea, defend the widow (Is 1:11-17).

It is no surprise that Christians who are ignorant of the role of the Holy Spirit in their spiritual life, do not relish the word of God. They feel no desire to know Scripture, nor the need of nourishing themselves on it. For them the Bible is a sealed book, a dead letter. Without the Holy Spirit, one does not comprehend God's message to us. It is not enough that Christ left us his message and examples. We must understand them, and this is the work of the Holy Spirit. Our Lord forewarned: "These things I have spoken to you while yet dwelling with you. But the Advocate, the Holy Spirit whom the Father will send in my name, he will teach all things, and bring to your mind whatever I have said to you" (Jn 14:25-26) "Many things yet I have to say to you, but you cannot bear them now. But when he, the Spirit of truth comes, he will teach you all the truth. For he will not speak on his own authority, but whatever he will hear he will speak, and the things that are to come he will declare to you" (16:12-13).

Thus deformed, destitute of all vitality, the Christian religion becomes tiresome and dull. It offers no attraction to people outside. Yet Christians have been charged by their Master to give witness to the glad tidings of salvation brought by him to the world. They should feel an urgent need to cry out their beliefs in order to make others share them. The well-being of all men is at stake. Christians who will not let themselves be led by the Holy Spirit are incapable of giving witness to the faith, because this witness can be only given through the power of the Spirit, as our Lord told his disciples: "You shall receive power when the Holy Spirit comes upon you and you shall be witnesses for me in Jerusalem and in all Judea and Samaria and even to the very ends of the earth" (Ac 1:8).

Because the religion of many Christians is not vivified by the Holy Spirit, and has changed into a moralism, legalism and formalism, there are today so many falling away. Many sincere persons, whether baptized or not, naturally religious and athirst for the Absolute and for intimacy with God, confronted with the deformed religion of too many Catholics, turn away from the Church and join Oriental religions and sects of all sorts, which today abound. There they hope to find what will satisfy their religious yearnings.

The baneful results stemming from ignorance of the Holy Spirit and of his primordial role in the practice of the Christian religion affect not only the spiritual and moral life of the faithful but also the Church, insofar as she is a human institution. The historical truth must be recognized that the Church-as-Institution, which is inhabited by the Holy Spirit as much as she is by the Body of Christ, has put the Spirit "in prison," so to say. Both in the past and even at the present, often too much stress is put on her institutional and hierarchical structures. And this human (institutional) aspect of the Church with its many laws and prescriptions, commandments and interdicts, has dominated the life and conduct of Catholics. The Church of Christ has taken the posture of a juridical society, she who should be a community of supernatural faith, hope and love.

A Church which severs herself from the life-giving action of the Spirit becomes an atrophic and sclerotic institution. Such a Church does not attract unbelievers and more seriously alienates her own children. That explains the words that are heard frequently today: "Christ yes, the Church no!"

Reasons for the Lack of Appreciation of the Holy Spirit

The ignorance of, or the lack of appreciation for the Holy Spirit is excusable, at least on the part of the faithful. Preachers rarely preach the Spirit in their talks, and rarely do the catechists in their catecheses. Catholic theology itself—Western theology—does not speak enough about the role of the Holy Spirit in the Church and in each Christian, in marked contrast to Eastern theology, both Catholic and Orthodox, and to Protestant theology, that have always done so.

It was a reproach that one of the Oriental Fathers, at Vatican II, His Excellency Monsignor Ziade, Maronite Archbishop of Beyrouth, addressed to the Latin Fathers. In his first intervention, in connection with the *Schema* on the Church, he said:

> *The Holy Spirit is almost completely absent in this chapter (on the People of God and on the laity especially). The Holy Spirit is indeed discussed in the first chapter of the Schema (up to #4), but in the course of the treatment, it does not come out sufficiently enough that it is his Presence which unifies the whole mystery of the Church. Now, according to Scripture and the constant Tradition of the Eastern Church, there is only one theology of the Church, and that is* pneumatic*: the Church is the mystery of the outpouring of the Spirit in "the last days" (Ac 2:17). The age of the Church in the history of salvation is called by the Fathers, "The Economy of the Spirit."*

The need to amend this chapter, and perhaps each chapter of the *Schema*, under the light of this central reality, appears to me for several reasons:

> (a) *In view of the renovation of the Church.* The theology of the Church evolved in the West more in relation with Christ and in a rather juridical manner, while in the East, it evolved in relation to the Holy Spirit and in a rather "mysterial" manner. The two aspects are complementary and shold be united. It appears to me that the moment has come to again take hold of all the traditional riches of the universal Church.

> (b) *In view of ecumenism.* It is in a fuller exposition of

the faith of this kind that we may be able at last to establish an understanding with our Eastern brothers, and recognize ourselves members of the same Church, one and indivisible, not only juridically but also, and above all, mystically.

(c) *In view of the pastoral ministry*. A more complete tradition explains more profoundly the missionary reality—historical, communal, sacramental and eschatalogical—of the People of God, during the age of the Church. The actual world, which considers, more often than not, the Church as a great sociological organization, and which nevertheless has a thirst for the Spirit of God, will not be thus frustrated in its expectations (Communication to the Council of Vatican II, on October 22, 1963).

The same prelate returned to this subject again in an intervention, in connection with the chapter about *Heaven,* by saying: "How is it possible to speak of our eschatalogical vocation without a mention of the Holy Spirit? We cannot recognize our Oriental tradition in a profession of faith so different." He then pointed out that "the Latin Ecclesiology grew exclusively in a Christological dimension, and it is still an adolescent in the Pneumatic (Spirit) dimenson." He concludes: "All the faithful, pastors above all, should live more and more the mystery of the Church, animated by the action of the Holy Spirit" (Msgr. Ignace Ziade, in *Doc. Cath* 4 Oct. 1964, Col 1239).

On this vital matter, Paul VI made this recommendation, in his Audience of June 6, 1973: "To Christology, and especially to the Christology of the Council, there must follow a new study and a new piety (fidelity) to the Holy Spirit precisely as an indispensable complement of the Council. "This new study and new fidelity has been greatly promoted for some years by the "charismatic renewal," about which I shall speak at the end of this book.

There are other reasons which excuse the lack of appreciation of the Holy Spirit. First of all, particular aspects of the modern world prevent people of this age from feeling the influence of the Spirit in their lives. Karl Rahner writes, "modern man lives under the sign of technology, of a managerial setup rationalized and planned by the mass media, of experimental psychology and psychoanalysis. In such environment, it is extremely difficult for one to discover, in the domain of his personal experience, an influence that he could describe as an action of the Holy Spirit. Everything appears profane in the material dialectics of cause and effect."

Another reason stems from the difficulty we meet in trying to conceive to ourselves the Third Person of the Holy Trinity. The Person of the Holy Spirit has an invisibility all his own. Not that the Father and the Son are not equally invisible to us. Indeed, invisibility is a radical attribute of each of the Three Persons. "No man," says St. Paul, "has seen or can see God who dwells in light inaccessible" (1 Tm 6:16). Nevertheless, for us it is less difficult to represent to ourselves the Father and the Son, if only because of their names. We know what is a human father or a human son. This knowledge gives us a glimpse, by analogy, of the personality of the Father in the heavens and of his divine Son. On the contrary, the name Spirit, which is that of the Third Person, does not call forth in our mind a human visage which would permit us to find in this Person a resemblance to our visible world. This name seems to us so abstract that it is difficult to understand that the Holy Spirit is a living person, with whom we can form a friendship.

In addition, the first Two Persons, the Father and the Son, invisible in their divine essence, have become visible, though each in a different manner.

The Son became visible by becoming man, like to man "in all things except sin" (Ph 2:7). It is therefore possible for us to see the invisible Person of the Son in "the man Jesus," the God-man, in whom the Son has revealed himself. As we believe, Jesus has only one *person*[ality] that of the Son of God. The mystery of the hypostatic union, basic Catholic dogma, is the union in the unique Person of the Son of the divine nature, which is common to him with the Father and the Holy Spirit, and the human nature, which he took in Mary's womb. His human nature reveals then to us his divine Person. Consequently, the human life, with its vicissitudes, activity, struggles and perils, as well as his human words and thoughts and the sentiments of his human heart, reveal to us the visage of the Son, the Word, who "from the beginning" was turned toward the Father in a thrust of filial love; and makes known to us the characteristic note, the constitutive element of his divine personality: his quality of Son, his filiation.

The Father too became visible, not in himself, but in his Son-become-man, Jesus Christ, who is, as St. Paul says, "the image of God (i.e., the Father);" (2 Cor 4:4) who is "the brightness of God's glory and the image of his substance" (Heb 1:3). So we cannot only represent him in the visage of a human father, but also see him on the face of the Incarnate Word. St. Paul speaks of the "glory of God (i.e., of the divine nature of the Father) shining on the face of Christ Jesus" (2 Cor 4:6). Our Lord himself answered Philip, who had asked him to reveal his Father. "Dost thou not believe that I am in the Father and the Father in me?" (Jn 14:8-11). And to Thomas: "I am the way, and the truth, and the life. No one comes to the Father but through me. If you had known me, you would also have known my Father. And henceforth you do know him, and you have seen him" (14:6-7). The Son is the perfect image of the Father in the Holy Trinity. The Son is another Father, he is his *"alter ego."* Jesus Christ, the Son-become-man, is therefore the exact revelation of the Father. To see the Son is to see the Father.

It isn't the same with the Third divine Person. The Holy Spirit has not revealed himself in a human visage, as a father, or a mother, or a son. He reveals himself through his action in the history of the world. He intervenes in the unfolding of human history (secular history) as well as of the history of salvation (sacred history). "The Holy Spirit who, by a wondrous providence, directs the course of the world," we read in the Constitution, *Gaudium et spes,* "and renews the face of the earth, is present to this evolution (of the social order)." However, he intervenes and works his wonders only to bring about the salvation of man, in order that "the human family . . . may be brought by the grace of Christ and the power of the Holy Spirit to the sublime and unending freedom of the glory of the sons of God" (Declaration of Religious Freedom, *Dignitatis humanae,* No. 15). It is by the effects of this salvific action that the Holy Spirit makes himself known. His visage is caught only in his wonders, gifts and charisms.

The Holy Spirit has revealed his action through various symbols. To limit ourselves to the New Testament, we learn that on the day of the Annunciation, the Spirit came upon Mary as a *Cloud* to overshadow her with its shade. At the Baptism of Jesus, the Spirit descended upon him as a *dove.* At Pentecost, the Spirit filled the Cenacle with a sound as of a violent *wind,* and his descent upon each of the Disciples showed itself as so many tongues of *fire,* and acted upon them in the manner of new *wine,* since they acted as if they were inebriated. Our Lord called the Spirit *living water.* These symbols, as we shall see later, permit to shine through them something of the Spirit's personality, by enlightening us on his way of acting, and by making us know the effects of his action. Nevertheless, none of these symbols possess the richness of a human visage, which would aid us to realize that the Holy Spirit is really a person.

The fact that the Holy Spirit has not revealed himself under human traits makes us realize that God is utterly above anything that our senses, imagination and spirit can know about him. That the Spirit surpasses infinitely human images shows that God is the Wholly-Other; in other words the particular invisibility of the Spirit shows the transcendental nature of God. It is the Spirit who realizes God's immanence in us; who makes the Son and the Father dwell in us. The Holy Spirit—sent in the world by the Father and the Son under the sensible form of *fire* and in us in a spiritual manner— obtains for us the interior and permanent presence in us of the Son and, with the Son, the presence of the Father. "If anyone love me," Our Lord says, "he will keep my word, and my Father will love him, and we will come and make our abode with him" (Jn 14:23).

As we shall see later, the Holy Spirit is the Person of the Holy Trinity who animates our whole spiritual being. Many movements of our soul which we are wont to ascribe to our nature are in reality activated through his impulses. He is the breathing of our heart, its breath of love; he it is who inspires our highest thoughts, illuminates our intelligence, enlightens our conscience, guides our will in the paths of the good, arouses our good desires. And every time that we love with a true love, that we entertain good desires and elevated thoughts, we do better than if we recognized him under a human visage. Talking to his disciples about the Holy Spirit, Jesus said: "I will ask the Father and he will give you another Advocate to dwell with you forever, the Spirit of truth whom the world cannot receive, because it neither sees him nor knows him. But you shall know him, because he will dwell with you, and be in you" (Jn 14:16-17).

"If then the Holy Spirit is invisible," writes Dom Vonier, "it is not in the sense that his presence is not evident. On the contrary, the characteristic of the Spirit, in the New Testament, is to be a manifest power, not a hidden and imperceptible force."

However paradoxical the statement may sound, the Holy Spirit is at the same time the divine Person most distant from us by his invisibility and the nearest to us. The paradox disappears when one discovers that the Spirit is Love in Person (personified). Love is that drive in us which is the most hidden in its being and the most involved by its action. Because the Holy Spirit is Love, he is the most invisible of the divine Persons but at the same time, he is the Person who enters in the deepest depths of our being and makes us live the love he is.

It is possible for us to know the person of the Holy Spirit, so invisible, so mysterious, so abstract, so blurred for a superficial look, but full of life and dynamic power for a contemplative gaze.

CHAPTER TWO

The Holy Spirit in the Holy Trinity

To contemplate the Holy Spirit in the Holy Trinity demands necessarily a study of the Trinitarian mystery itself, the mystery of the inner life of God. However, since the aim of this chapter is centered on the Holy Spirit, envisaged itself in his relation to this mystery, my treatment on the Trinitarian mystery itself will be intentionally limited.

The mystery of the inner life of God was revealed by Jesus Christ. St. John having affirmed that "no one has at any time seen God," adds immediately: "The only-begotten Son, who is in the bosom of the Father, he has revealed him" (Jn 1:18). Only the Son could do so, since only he knows God because "he is from the Father and was sent by him" (Jn 7:29), according to Jesus' own words.

This revelation tells us that God is a living God, whose life is an exchange of love among Three Persons, the Father, the Son and the Holy Spirit. The Three Persons communicate each to the other Two all that they are and all that they have, possessing but one and the same nature (essence or substance), and distinguish Themselves, One from the Other Two by the manner Each possesses and gives their unique nature, which is love itself, according to the astounding declaration of St. John that "God is Love" (1 Jn 4:8).

The Holy Spirit, The Personal Love of the Father and the Son

Let us try to penetrate this wondrous mystery. To do that, I will start from an analogy, taken from Scripture itself, namely, that of the human spirit.

When God created man, he said that he would make him "according to his image and likeness" (Gn 1:26). God being pure Spirit, it is our spirit—the spiritual principle that animates our whole being and which is made up essentially of two faculties, intelligence and will, which enables us to know and to love—it is our spirit that has been created to the "image and likeness" of God. This biblical verse permits us to seek in our spirit the traces of God: the One God in Three Persons.

What follows is rather abstract and difficult to follow, yet it is necessary to go in these theoretical subtleties if we want to learn something about the Holy Trinity.

I ascertain, first of all, that my spirit *is,* that it is *one,* and that it is precisely *spiritual.* We have here already something in common with the Triune God, who *Is,* who is *One,* and who is a *Spiritual Being.* I next observe that my spirit *thinks;* that thinking it conceives (or constructs) a *thought.* When it thinks a thing other than itself, it conceives a thought like (or similar to) this thing, for the thought becomes like the object thought. Now if my spirit thinks about itself, it conceives a thought similar to itself. My spirit then feels that the thought (construct) that it has of itself, is *identical* to it (my spirit), because the mental construct is an expression of what my spirit is. At the same time, although the thought remains in my spirit, even when it is expressed exteriorly, the spirit feels it to be *distinct,* since in the spirit that thinks there is something more than in the spirit that does not think. Hence there are *two:* the spirit that conceives, the father of the construct, and the thought, the offspring of the spirit—what we call its *mental word,* or interior word because the spirit speaks it within itself before the thought bcomes exterior through the *spoken word.* Analogically then, the human spirit corresponds to God the Father, the mental word (thought or construct) to God the Son, to the Word before the Incarnation.

If my spirit thinks all of himself, its thought, embracing it (my spirit) wholly, will be, though engendered by it, equal to it, and my spirit will recognize in its thought all of himself. He will gaze at this thought with its rich and engaging qualities, and will admire it, since it expresses the perfections of my spirit. My spirit will then be satisfied with it. This movement of (selfsatisfaction) is *love.* My spirit will love it. Since it is wholly itself that the spirit conceives, it will love all of itself thus conceived; its love will embrace its whole thought.

If this thought, instead of being (as in us) an unsubstantial modality of our spirit, could elevate itself to be (as in God) a living person—aware of self and capable of knowing and of loving—it (the thought) would gaze back at the spirit which has conceived it, and recognizing itself in it (in the spirit) as the source of the perfections that it expresses, it (the thought) would love its conceiver (begetter) with the same love that the begetter (the father) loves it. And since the thought embraces the whole spirit, out of which it issued, it would love the whole spirit.

The love of the spirit for its thought and the reciprocal love of the thought for the spirit, embracing the whole thought and the whole spirit, would be as great as the spirit, and though this love would be distinguishable from the one and the other, it would remain with both, since the spirit and its thought would be one into the other. This love which would proceed from the one and the other, and which would tie the one to the other, without blending with them, would correspond to God the Holy Spirit, and would complete this miniature human trinity.

This is one of the rational explanations the human intellect can give of the mystery of the Holy Trinity, on the authority of the verse of Genesis: "God said: Let us make man in our image and likeness." Now, let us try to acquire a better knowledge of this wondrous secret of God, which Our Lord has revealed to us.

My study will be unavoidably an abstract. I'm afraid that it may even appear to some as play on words! Not at all, for what I am going to say on this subject has a basis in the reality such as known by us through revelation. It will not be an experiential knowledge of God; experiential knowledge is not the fruit of philosophical speculation but of the exercise of the theological virtues and the gifts of the Holy Spirit.

Being a pure Spirit, God cannot be perceived either by our senses or by our imagination; he can only be known analogically by a spiritual faculty, our intellect. The knowledge of God in his Trinitarian life that we have here in view is, accordingly, an intellectual and speculative knowledge. A knowledge of this kind can only be theoretical, since it is the fruit of a work of intellectual reflection, which uses pure ideas whose verbal expressions will be inevitably abstract. Nevertheless, this knowledge does enlighten one who applies himself to attain it provided that to the *intellectual* study of the mystery follows the *experience* of God.

You may give courses to young people on love, marriage, the psychology of man and of woman, sexuality, and so forth; the result will be that the young people will have an adequate, even deep, knowledge of these subjects, but it will be theoretical. It will lack an essential element: experience. To have a complete knowledge they need the experience of love: they must marry, live their love. Only then will they have an experimental knowledge of conjugal love, which will perfect their theoretical knowledge. Yet, this latter will not remain less necessary and indispensable for the success of their marriage. They obtain also the knowledge of God and of the relations between God and man, which the Bible in fact compares to a human marriage, to conjugal love. An intellectual knowledge of the mystery of God, while necessary, is absolutely inadequate for a full supernatural understanding: we need an experiential knowledge of God, we must live his Trinitarian life. But this is the personal affair of a Christian, aided by the Holy Spirit.

The God, of whom Jesus speaks as his Father, is a God who has "life in himself" (Jn 5:26), who possesses this life in absolute fullness. Now, this plenitude of life cannot be conceived without thought and love. These two vital operations belong to God the Father by necessity of his nature, and in him are so immense and extraordinary that they are Two divine Persons, who well up from God's bosom, without leaving it. In God, there are in addition to the Father two other Persons, who are the perfect expression and complement of his inner life. They are the fruit of the return of the Father on himself, to think himself, to love his thought and to be loved by it. These Persons are uniquely spirits, so their acts are uniquely spiritual: they know and they love. They do nothing else but to know and love Each Other.

Having the fullness of life and of being, in an absolute manner—for the *Living* par excellence is *Being Itself,* is *He Who Is*—the Father knows and thinks of himself as necessary, otherwise, he would not really be. In knowing himself, he knows himself as he is: the Father's thought corresponds fully with himself and expresses him totally, without any mingling. Like us and infinitely better than us, the Father is conscious of what he is; he represents himself to himself; and in this representation, perfect as is perfect all that happens in him, he begets Another himself. He utters silently this thought of himself in the bosom of the Godhead. "The Father utters only one word," says St. John of the Cross, "and this word is his Son. He utters it always in an eternal silence that the soul hears." This thought is the Word, who forms a Reality as perfect and conscious as the Father, a Person like him: his Son to whom he communicates his nature and all his perfections, except that of being Father.

In contemplating his infinite perfections, the Father thus begets his Son; and it is this Son that he contemplates, since his Son is his exact image: "the splendor of his glory," and "the imprint of his substance," and in him finds himself all entire. Seeing himself in his Son, as in a clear mirror, seeing himself in another who possesses everything he possesses, finds delight in him: he cannot but be pleased with him and love him.

The Son, being the expression of the Father, personifies Absolute Beauty, Truth and Goodness, in a word, the Sovereign Good which is the Father. Every good by its very nature provokes necessarily the love of desire in those who know of it, because it can fill a need in them; this love finds its fulfillment in the love of delight in the good possessed. The Father, therefore, loves his Son necessarily with the love of desire, because he finds in him his good, the possibility to be what he is, i.e., Father, or the principle of the Sovereign Good which the Son is, as the Begotten of the Father. He desires his Son because he has "need" of him to be Father. This "need" does not constitute an imperfection in him, since it does not mean a lack in him. It simply expresses the very demand of his Person, without which he would not be Father. The Father exists only for his Son, and that is why he has for his Son a total welcome.

The love of the Father reposes itself in his well-beloved Son and finds his delight, not less necessarily. At the Baptism of Jesus and at the Transfiguration, the Father will declare: "This is my beloved Son in whom I am well pleased." The love of desire and of delight flow both from another kind of love: the love as a gift. For love is not only a pleasant welcome of the beloved, it is also the gift of self which the lover makes to his beloved. As in human love, so it is with divine love.

Though the Father has *need* of his Son to be Father, yet he first gives him the *gift* to be Son, by begetting him. The Father finds *delight* in his Son, because he contemplates his whole essence in the Son. The Father's essence which the Son possesses wholly, is given by the Father from all eternity. For all eternity and always he has a Son, since he cannot be Father unless he has a Son; that he possesses his Being only to communicate it to his Son, that he exists only for his Son, that he is Father only in giving himself totally to his Son. Therefore, the Father loves necessarily his Son, has need of, and finds in him delight, with an eternal, infinite and self-giving love.

The Son, on his part, because he is a person, and hence capable of knowledge and love, contemplates in the bosom of the Godhead, the infinite perfections of his Father, of whom he is the perfect expression; he finds in his Father the principle and source of the infinite Beauty, Truth and Goodness which he (the Son) personifies. This knowledge carries him toward his Father in a reflective impetus (*elan*) of love: a love of desire and of delight, but also a love of acknowledgment for the Father's total gift of himself. Finally, a love which propels him in return to make the total gift of himself to his Father.

The Father loves the Son and the Son returns this love to the Father. Now their mutual love—which is also unique, for it is the same love with which the Father loves the Son and the Son loves the Father—constitutes a Third Person, who is the Holy Spirit.

Generally, people have considerable difficulty accepting this affirmation: that the Holy Spirit, otherwise called *Love,* is a Person. Revelation shows the Spirit as a person, for it speaks of someone who accomplishes acts which belong to a person. "I will ask the Father," Jesus said, "and he will give you another Advocate (like Jesus, who is a person) to dwell with you forever, the Spirit of truth whom the world cannot receive, because it neither sees him nor knows him. But you shall know him, because he will dwell with you and be in you" (Jn 14:16-17). "These things I have spoken to you while yet dwelling with you. But the Advocate, the Holy Spirit, whom the Father will send in my name, he will teach you all things, and bring to your mind whatever I have said to you" (14:25-26). "Many things yet I have to say to you, but you cannot bear them now. But when he, the Spirit of truth, has come, he will teach you all the truth. For he will not speak on his own authority, but whatever he will hear he will speak, and the things that are to come he will declare to you" (16:12-13). St. Paul says that "the Spirit searches all things, even the deep things of God" (1 Cor 2:10); and our Lord said that "the Spirit (like the wind) blows where he wills" (Jn 3:8). These are acts of the intellect and will, therefore they are *personal* acts.

The Holy Spirit, who searches "the deep things of God," contemplates in the Son the infinite perfections of the Father, whose exact expression he is. "The Spirit will receive what is mine;" "All things that the Father has are mine" (Jn:14-15). And this knowledge of the One and the Other, makes the Spirit love the Father and the Son, the Father by the Son and the Son by the Father, with the same love with which they love each other and which is no other than he himself. The Father and the Son contemplate each other in their common Spirit, somewhat like the human father and mother who see each other in looking at their child. The Son contemplates his image in the Holy Spirit. The Father in the same Spirit contemplates the image of his Son. Finally this contemplation takes the Father and the Son toward the Holy Spirit with a love, which is not different from the love with which they love Each Other, and this love is the Holy Spirit.

The Holy Spirit is therefore a person like the Father and the Son. What constitutes the divine Persons as such are the *relations* which exist among Them. The Father is only a father because he has a Son. He exists only (for) or relatively to his Son, to whom he gives all that he is, except his Paternity. This paternal relation constitutes the personality of the Father. The Son is all that the Father is but he is not a father. Likewise, the Son is only a son because he has a father. He exists only relatively to his Father. The Father is all that the Son is, but he is not a son. Only the Filial relation constitutes the personality of the Son. The Holy Spirit too is constituted (a Person) by a relation, that to his unique origin: the Father-Son. He is only the infinite Breath of Love, which proceeds from the One and the Other, as from a unique source, and in which he communicates to Them—to the Son by the Father and to the Father by the Son—all that he is except his Procession. And only this Procession, the Breath of Love, constitutes the personality of the Holy Spirit.

These relations, while constituting the divine Persons as such, distinguish at the same time Each from the Two Others, for there can be no relations except among distinct beings. Hence, the Paternal relation distinguishes the Father from the Son; the Filial relation, the Son from the Father; and the Procession of Love, the Holy Spirit from the Father and the Son.

Notwithstanding the real distinction which exists among the Three Persons, there is among them a union no less real, a union which is more than a union: a *unity*. Since there is only One God, the Oneness of the Godhead unites the Persons of the Holy Trinity in a unity the most complete, for the relations which constitute the divine persons as such, and consequently the Persons themselves, are not distinguished from the divine nature, from the divine Being who is Love Itself. Each is identified with this substantial Love, and Each possesses the same and only Love. The first is the love possessed and given by the Father, as principle and source: paternal love. The second is the love possessed and returned by the Son, as generated by the father: filial love. The third is the love possessed and given and returned by the Holy Spirit, as proceeding from the Father and the Son: the personal love, the paterno-filial love, the same love which makes the Father and the Son exist only for each other.

Being identical to the same and unique nature, the divine Persons are united among themselves in connection with this nature, while Each is distinguished from the Other Two by their relations. They are present to Each Other; they dwell Each in the Other Two. This is why Our Lord could say to Philip: "Don't you believe that I am in the Father and the Father is in me?" (Jn 14:10).

This reciprocal presence or indwelling in Each Other is not an ordinary abode and rest. An intense circulation of love vibrates this abode of the divine Persons. The relations which constitute the divine Persons, while distinguishing One from the Others, carries them along, propels Each toward the other Two, in a movement of love so intense that it gives Each to the other Two and unites them in the most perfect unity. Thus that which distinguishes the divine Persons, i.e., their reciprocal relations: Paternal, Filial, Paterno-filial, is at the same time what unites them These relations are those of knowledge and of love. They arise from the knowledge by the Father of the Son, and that of the Father by the Son, and this mutual knowledge reaches completion in the mutual love of the Father and the Son consummated in the ineffable embrace of the Holy Spirit.

The Holy Spirit is Love personified. The activity of love in God is so intense that it results in a new Person. The love that the Father has for his Son and the Son has for his Father is so strong, so complete that it separates itself from the Two, in some way, to constitute a distinct Person. The Holy Spirit subsists only as Love. He is the personal and living expression of the Love which is God.

St. Augustine, who was one of the very first to have discovered Love as the essential characteristic of the Holy Spirit, writes:

> *(The Holy Spirit is) their common Spirit. What does that mean? Is it their unity with each other, their holiness, their love? their substantial and eternal communion? their friendship and fellowship? Yes, we say, it is their mutual charity, the love of the Father for the Son and the Son for the Father. It is this reciprocal and essential gift that they preserve between them the unity of the Spirit in the bond of peace. Thus we know that there can only be three: he who loves his offspring, he who loves his principle, and their love* (De Trinitate, Book VI, n. 7).

The mystery of the personification of love which is the Holy Spirit becomes clear in the light of the psychology of human love, which shows that love is essentially unitive; it yearns for the union of the beings which it affects. Plato's ideas on this subject are well-known. He writes in *The Symposium:*

> *Suppose Hephaestus with his tools were to visit lovers as they love each other, and asks them: "What is it, mortals, that you hope to gain from one another?" Suppose too that when they could not answer he repeated his question in these terms: "Is the object of your desire to be always together as much as possible, and never be separated from one another day or night? If that is what you want, I am ready to melt and weld you together, so that, instead of two, you shall be one flesh; as long as you live you shall live a common life, and when you die, you shall suffer a common death, and be still one, not two, even in the next world. Would such a fate as this content you, and satisfy your longings?" We know what their answer would be; no one would refuse the offer; it*

> *would be plain that this is what everybody wants, and everybody would regard it as the precise expression of the desire which he had long felt but had been unable to formulate, that he should melt into his beloved, and that thenceforth they should be one instead of two. (The Symposium Penguin Books, pp. 63-64).*

Every true love carries a longing for ecstasy, in the etymological meaning of the term: a going out of oneself. It urges lovers to come out of themselves and go into each other. It carries them further than themselves: with the "me and you" it makes them beyond themselves a "us," which is a product of their mutual love.

Divine love too carries in itself this desire. And only it can realize it in all truth and perfection. In loving each other, the Father and the Son come out of themselves, as it were, and form beyond their love a reality, which to be perfect as is perfect all that is in God, constitutes a Person like them: the Person of the Holy Spirit.

The Holy Spirit is the personified ecstasy of the Father and the Son. Far from being an abstract person without luster and life, he is the very personification of exaltation and enthusiasm, of inebriation and joy, of vitality and dynamic energy. Consequently, the Holy Spirit is the song of the Father and the Son, their common jubilation and joy, which well up from their blessedness in giving Each Other a gift of themselves, in loving in being loved. He is their kiss that seals, in the indivisible unity of the divine nature, the Three divine Persons in an eternal ecstasy of infinite joy.

The Holy Spirit, "the living weight of happiness in the heart of God bent over the Object of his love," (as A.M. Henry, O.P., writes) is represented among other symbols by that of *oil,* which is considered as a sign of joy in the Bible: "the oil of gladness." God's joy is a joy completely disinterested, untouched by egoism. With us humans the joy of love is unavoidably and invariably marked by greater or less egoism: our search for the personal well-being which we experience in loving and being loved makes us selfish. With God the risk of personal egoism does not exist. In the personal gift that the Three divine Persons make to Each Other there can be no egoism. In fact, the Father does not love himself, nor does the Son love himself. St. Bonaventure says: "The Love who is the Holy Spirit does not proceed from the Father insofar as the Father loves himself; nor from the Son insofar as the Son loves himself; but it proceeds from their loving one another. It is a bond; it is the love by which the lover turns towards the beloved." There is no egoism *by two* either, since the mutual love of the Father and the Son does not stop itself at them; it does not close itself upon them as in a closed society. On the contrary, it ends or results in the production of a Third Person to whom the Other two communicate their whole Being. The Procession of the Holy Spirit, Richard of St. Victor says, "is like the free outpouring between two friends, the Father and the Son, who in their generosity agree to communicate to a third the joy of being loved as they love each other."

Names and Attributes of the Third Divine Person

Why is the Third Person of the Trinity called the Holy Spirit, why the name Spirit? The Third Person of the Trinity is called Spirit not because he is immaterial, i.e., exempt of all matter, or pure spirit. Understood thus, spirit would not be the proper name of the Third divine Person, since also the Father is a spirit and the Son. The term must be taken in its etymological meaning, which is a translation of the Tebrew *ruah,* of the Greek *pneuma,* of the Latin *spiritus* and of the Arab *rouah.* And it means *breath;* at the same time it means also *soul.* Our Lord himself understood it thus. He compared the Holy Spirit to the breath of the wind. Alluding to the Spirit, he said to Nicodemus: "The wind blows where it will, and thou hearest its sound but dost not know where it comes from or where it goes" (Jn 3:8). After his Resurrection, he appeared to his disciples and breathed upon them saying: "Receive the Holy Spirit" (Jn 20:22).

Why this symbol? According to St. Thomas, the word *spirit* evokes in the world of matter a kind of impulsion and motion. Now, it is the nature of love to move and impel the will of the lover towards the beloved. St. Thomas sees the note of impulsion, of interior *elan,* of movement in which is life *(vita in motu)* at the base of the notion of spirit, and which has given the name Spirit to the Third Person of the Trinity.

> *The beloved exists in the will as an inclination which draws the will as a force which in some way intrinsically impels the lover towards the beloved. Now, in all living things the impulse which comes from within liberates the breath or vital spirit. This is why it is fitting that God, who proceeds by way of love, bear the name Spirit, since he proceeds by way of breath or spiration. This is why St. Paul attributes to the Spirit and to Love a certain power of impulsion: Those who are the sons of God, are led by the Spirit, he says to the Romans (8:14). nd to the Corinthians: "The charity of Christ presseth us" (2 Cor 5:14) (Contra Gentiles).*

Isn't the Holy Spirit the very movement of divine life? Doesn't the deep life of the Father and the Son breathe in him, as the life of man inhales the breath which makes him live, the breath of life that God "breathed in his nostrils?" (Gn 2:7). Now, in God, life is identical with love. God lives only by love because he is Love. The Holy Spirit is the full personal expression of divine love. Since God is love in its fullness, and since love in such an extreme degree doesn't talk or sing any longer, and only exhales a sigh or breath into which the soul pours itself wholly, it was suitable to symbolize the Third divine Person by the breath and to give him the name of Spirit. He is the breath of love of the Father and the Son.

We say of the Father and of the Son, as of the human father and mother, that they are love, in the sense that they love each other. Love indicates the act of the will towards the loved object. In this sense St. John writes that "God is love." We say further of the Father and the Son only, as of the human father and mother only, that they are love, in the sense that in loving each other they produce the fruit of their love: the Holy Spirit or the human child. Love then indicates the production of love and applies in a common fashion, but exclusively to the Father and to the Son, to the human father and mother. Finally we say of the Holy Spirit only, as of the child only that he is love, in this sense that he is the fruit proceeding from two beings who love each other, and who say to each other, "our love." The term Love (or the Holy Spirit) indicates then the sigh or the breath of love of the Father and the Son. It is in this last sense that love is the proper name of the Holy Spirit—and as such it has always been understood by Tradition.

Breath of divine love, the name Spirit also signifies the depths of this love. The breath (or sigh) wells up from the depths of a being. So the Holy Spirit expresses and opens up what is deepest in the Father and the Son, what is most intimate in them. The term spirit also symbolizes the vivifying power of the Holy Spirit, his power of penetration. He permeates by his presence every being in whom he dwells. For this other reason he is represented by the symbol of oil, and this element is used in the Holy Chrism.

The word spirit, as we have already seen, indicates the wind, of which Our Lord said: "The wind blows where it will and you hear its sound but do not know where it comes from or where it goes. So is everyone who is born of the Spirit" (Jn 3:18). The term is apt to symbolize the freedom of the Holy Spirit, who St. Paul says, "allots to everyone according as he wills" (1 Cor 12:11). Free, the Holy Spirit communicates freedom to Christians: "Where the Spirit of the Lord is, there is freedom" (2 Cor 3:17). We become free in the measure we are docile to the impulses and to the action of the Holy Spirit.

The wind symbolizes the Holy Spirit also for its force, as well as for the gentleness with which it blows. The wind can blow with force. That is why the name symbolizes the power of the Holy Spirit. He is, in fact, described by Scripture as being the power of God, inasmuch as he is the expression of the life of God and is the breath of divine love. Human love is said to be, "as strong as death" (Sg 8:6). All the more it must be said of divine love, of the Spirit of Love: he is the personified power of God. Thus it is to the Holy Spirit that Scripture attributed the mighty works of God. *Creation:* "The Spirit of God was stirring above the waters" (Gn 1:2). *Incarnation:* "The Holy Spirit shall come upon thee," said the angel Gabriel to Mary, "and the power of the Most High shall overshadow thee" (Lk 1:35). *The Resurrection of Jesus Christ and ours:* "But if the Spirit of him who raised Jesus, Jesus Christ from the dead dwells in you," St. Paul writes, "then he who raised Jesus Christ from the dead will bring to life your mortal bodies because of his Spirit who dwells in you" (Rm 8:11). *The transformation of the Apostles and Christians to make them witnesses of Christ:* "You shall receive power when the Holy

Spirit comes upon you, and you shall be witnesses for me" (Ac 1:8). Our Lord told his disciples announcing to them the near coming of the Spirit. When the Spirit did come on Pentecost, he came "as of a violent wind blowing" (Ac 2:2). The Liturgy attributes to the power of the Holy Spirit the transformation of the substance of bread and wine into the Body and Blood of Jesus Christ, as well as our own transformation. Nevertheless, the wind can also blow with gentleness, and then it symbolizes the discreet and quiet manner with which the Spirit ordinarily penetrates human hearts—as the breath of light breeze.

It remains for us to see why the Spirit of love is also called holy. Aren't the other Two Persons also holy? Certainly. However, the title is given to the Third in a special and personal manner. We must recall that holiness consists in the perfection of charity (love), the perfect practice of the commandment of love. Our Lord declared that the moral perfection of man, holiness in other words, lies in the love of God and the neighbor to which the whole Law and the Prophets are attached, since all other commandments are the manifold and varied expression of the one commandment of love. Now, Our Lord told us to imitate God in order to be perfect: "You therefore are to be perfect, even as your heavenly Father is perfect" (Mt 5:48). St. Paul did the same: "Be you, therefore, imitators of God, as very dear children, and walk in love, as Christ also loved us and delivered himself for us an offering and a sacrifice to God to ascend in fragrant odor" (Ep 5:12). If then man's moral perfection consists in love, much more does divine perfection. If the practice of love sanctifies man, it is because God's holiness stems from love, with which the Father and the Son love Each Other, i.e., the Holy Spirit. Since he is Love in person, the Spirit is called Holy. He is Holiness in person, and that is why he is the Sanctifier who makes us holy.

Holiness in person, the Holy Spirit makes us understand what is true holiness. In the Old Testament *holy* is synonymous with *separated.* God's holiness is in his *transcendence,* his infinite separation from all that is created. The Old testament revelation highlighted this aspect of the Godhead: The God who is the Wholly-Other, the *mysterium tremendum, tremenda majestas:* awe-full Reality which creates stupor and blank wonder in the creature. But there is another aspect of God, which though not unknown in the

Old, was revealed more fully in the New Testament: God as the *mysterium fascinans,* the God of joyous love, gracious mercy, pity and comfort. The Holy Spirit, as Love in person, is a wondrously apt figure of this aspect of God. The Spirit suitably gives to those who let themselves be transformed by him a sample, or "foretaste" of divine beatitude and of the "peace which surpasseth understanding."

The essence of holiness is love, and love is unitive. Separation is the means which permits love to effect the union of God with his creatures, without blending the Creator and the creatures. The Holy Spirit makes us understand that holiness separates from the world those whom he sanctifies but only to unite them to God. Likewise it separates them from sinners only to gather them all together, without the ones acquiring the sins of the others. Consequently, holiness is not isolation from the world, a "flight from the world," nor is it maceration of the body, but is a Spirit-infused love which expands one to the full dimension of the world, and makes us imitators of God.

The Holy Spirit is also called *Paraclete,* a name given to him by Our Lord himself. St. John is the only New Testament writer who employed the term: four times in his Gospel and once in his First Epistle. The Latin translation of the Vulgate kept the Greek word *Parakletos* of the Johannine Gospel, but in the First Epistle the Vulgate translates the word *Parakletos, Advocate. Advocate* renders better the meaning of the Greek term which means: a call to, a call for asking advice, a call to one's aid or defense, an appeal to. Hence, the term is better translated *Advocate* than *Consoler,* traditionally used, though the thought of *consolation* is not lacking.

In his Discourse after the Last Supper, Our Lord called the Holy Spirit the Paraclete: "I will ask the Father and he will give you another Advocate to dwell in you forever, the Spirit of truth" (Jn 14:16): "The Advocate, the Holy Spirit, whom the Father will send in my name, will teach you all things and bring to your mind whatever I have said to you" (14:26). "When the Advocate has come, whom I will send from the Father, the Spirit of truth which proceeds from the Father will bear witness concerning me" (15:26); "If I do not go, the Advocate will not come to you" (1:7). And in his First Letter, St. John says: "If anyone sins, we have an Advocate with the Father, Jesus Christ, the Just" (1 Jn 2:1).

Telling his disciples, when about to go away from them, that the Father would send them another Advocate, Our Lord showed that during the time he was with them, he was their Advocate, but that after his departure, the Holy Spirit would be their Advocate, and forever. As for Jesus, once he ascended to the heavens, he has been our Advocate before the Father, interceding for us. St. Paul writes: "Christ Jesus is at the right hand of God and intercedes for us" (Rm 8:34); and in Hebrews, we read that Christ "has an everlasting priesthood and is therefore able at all times to save those who come to God through him, since he lives always to make intercession for them" (7:24-25).

A last term, which completes the revelation of the personality of the Holy Spirit, is that of *Gift,* "by which the sacred writers and Christian Tradition characterize the Third Person of the Trinity, taking their inspiration from Our Lord, who said, for example: "if evil as you are, know how to give good gifts to your children, how much more will your heavenly Father give the Good Spirit to those who ask him" (Lk 11:13). St. Paul will say to the Romans: "The love of God is poured forth in our hearts by the Holy Spirit who has been given to us as a gift" (Rm 5:5). Echoing to what Christ said to the Samaritan woman, "If you knew the gift of God" (Jn 4:10) St. Peter will depict the Holy Spirit by this simple term, Gift: "Repent and be baptized every one of you in the name of Jesus Christ for the forgiveness of your sins and you will receive the gift of the Holy Spirit" (Ac 2:38). On another occasion, St. Peter will call the Holy Spirit "the gift of God" (Ac 8:20). St. Luke will say, narrating the baptism of the first pagans: "While Peter was speaking these words, the Holy Spirit came upon all who were listening to his message. And the faithful of the circumcision, who had come with Peter, were amazed, because on the Gentiles also the gift of the Holy Spirit had been poured forth" (Ac 10:44-45).

The Liturgy, in one of its numerous beautiful hymns, the sequence: *Veni Creator,* calls the Holy Spirit, the "Gift of God most high":

> *Come, Spirit, Creator, Visit the souls of those who are yours;*
> *fill with grace from on high the hearts you have created.*

> *You who are named Paraclete, Gift of God most high, living*
> *Spring, Fire, Love, spiritual Unction.*
> *You are the sevenfold Gift, the Finger of God's right hand;*
> *you are the solemn promise of the Father;*
> *you enrich our mouths with the gift of the Word.*
> *Enkindle a light in our mind, pour love into our hearts, and*
> *fortify with constant vigor the weakness of our bodies.*
> *Push the enemy far from us, and give us continuous peace;*
> *so that being guarded by you*
> *we may avoid all that is harmful.*
> *Grant that through you we may know the Father*
> *as well as the Son, and that we may believe at all times,*
> *in you, the Spirit of them both.*
> *Glory to the Father and to the Son and to the Holy Spirit,*
> *and may the Son send us the Gifts of the Spirit.*

The Holy Spirit is the first Gift given to man by the Father and the
Son, according to St. Thomas:

> *A gift, properly speaking, is a giving without anything in*
> *return, i.e., a giving without the hope of reward. A true gift*
> *implies gratuity. Now, for what reason do we give*
> *gratuitously unless it be that we love? If, in fact, we do give*
> *something gratuitously to another, it is because we desire his*
> *well-being, which is another way of saying that we love him.*
> *So the first thing we give him is love in as much as we desire*
> *his well-being. Thus love is the first gift in virtue of which all*
> *gratuitous gifts are given. And since it is established that the*
> *Holy Spirit proceeds as Love he proceeds also as a first gift.*
> *St. Augustine says: "The particular gifts which are*
> *distributed to the members of Christ come from the GIFT*
> *which is the Holy Spirit"* (Summa Theol. Ia, qu 38, art. 2).

The Holy Spirit is the Gift *par excellence* for us, because, as we have
seen , he is the total Gift in the bosom of the Trinity: the total Love
Gift that the Father gives to the Son, and the Son in return gives to the
Father.

Love brings *enrichment* to both lover and beloved if they are ready to *impoverish* themselves by giving each to the other. Thus it is in God: the *reciprocal* love of the Father and of the Son reaches to the point of total "impoverishment," or of the total loss of the One in the Other. It is only in giving himself totally to the Son that the Father realizes his personality (divine Paternity); it is the same with the Son, and he realizes his divine Filiation. And their total giving makes a Third Person to well up in the bosom of God. It is the same inhuman love: the gift of oneself enriches one's personality greatly: it *personalizes.*

What better way is there than to end this chapter on the attributes of the Holy Spirit with the sequence *Veni Sancte Spiritus* which, like the *Veni Creator* cited earlier, sings in beautiful verses the manifold and gracious gifts of the Holy Spirit:

> *Come, Holy Spirit, and send a ray of light from on high, Come, Father of the poor, Come, Giver of all gifts, Light of men's hearts. The best Comforter, delightful Guest of the Soul, sweet refreshment, Rest in toil, appeasement in the midday heart, Solace for tears. O blessed Light, fill in their inmost parts, the hearts of the faithful! Without your Favour, there is nothing in man, and nothing is guiltless. Wash what is soiled, water what is dry, heal what is wounded, Soften what is stiff, warm what is cold, direct what has strayed; Grant your faithful who confide in you the sevenfold and sacred gift; Grant the merit of virtue, grant a blessed end, grant eternal joy!*

CHAPTER THREE

The Holy Spirit in the Life of Christ

A little while before ascending to his Father, Christ said to his disciples: "I will send forth upon you the promise of my Father. But wait here in the city, until you are clothed with power from on high" (Lk 24:49). St. Luke, who has recorded these words of the Lord at the end of his Gospel, recalls them at the beginning of Acts: "While eating with his Apostles," he writes, "Jesus charged them not to depart from Jerusalem, but to wait for the promise of the Father, 'of which you have heard,' said he, 'by my mouth; for John indeed baptized with water, but you shall be baptized with the Holy Spirit not many days hence' " (Ac 1:4-5).

By telling his Apostles that they would be clothed with power from on high," and that they would "be baptized with the Holy Spirit," our Lord made them understand explicitly that it is the Holy Spirit who is, according to the expression of St. Peter, "the promise of the Father." A little later, he will tell them: "You shall receive power when the Holy Spirit comes upon you" (Ac 1:8). Accordingly, St. Paul will call the Holy Spirit: "the promise of the Spirit" (Gal 3:14); and "the Holy Spirit of the promise" (Ep 1:13).

When did God the Father make this promise? What are the words to which Christ alludes and by which the Father promised the Gift of the Spirit? He did so many times by his prophets.

In Isaiah, we read: "The Spirit from on high will be poured on us anew. Then will the desert become an orchard and the orchard be regarded as a forest" (32:15-16); "I will pour out water upon thirsty ground, and streams upon the dry land; I will pour out my Spirit upon your descendants" (44:3). "Remember not the events of the past, the things of long ago consider not; see, I am doing something new: Now it springs forth, do you not perceive it? In the desert I make a way, in the wasteland, rivers . . . I put water in the desert and rivers in the wasteland for my chosen people to drink" (43:18-21).

The prophet Jeremiah, foretelling the "New Covenant" in the Spirit, declared:

> *"The days are coming," says the Lord, "when I will make a new covenant with the house of Israel . . . It will not be like the covenant I made with their fathers the day I took them by the hand to lead them forth from the land of Egypt; for they broke my covenant". . . . "But this is the covenant which I will make with the house of Israel after those days," says the Lord. "I will place my law within them, and write it upon their hearts; I will be their God, and they shall be my people. No longer will they have need to teach their friends and kinsmen how to know the Lord. All, from least to greatest, shall know me," says the Lord (31:31-34).*

The Lord spoke again of the "New Covenant" through the prophet Ezechiel in these words: "I will give them a new heart and put a new spirit within them; I will remove the stony heart from their bodies, and replace it with a carnal heart, so that they will live according to my statutes, and observe and carry out my ordinances; thus they shall be my people and I will be their God" (11:19-21). Again: "I will sprinkle clean water to cleanse you. from all your impurities, and from all your idols I will cleanse you. I will give you a new heart and place a new spirit within you, taking from your bodies your stony hearts and giving you loving hearts. I will put my Spirit within you and make you live by my statutes, careful to observe my decrees" (Ezk 36:25-27). Ezechiel records this promise of the "New Covenant" two more times thus: "O my people! I will put my Spirit in you that you may live" (37:14); "No longer will I hide my face from them, for I have poured out my Spirit upon the house of Israel" (39:29).

Finally, the prophecy of Joel, cited by St. Peter, on the day of Pentecost: "Then afterwards I will pour my Spirit upon all mankind. Your sons and daughters shall prophesy, your old men shall dream dreams, your young men shall see visions; even upon the servants and the handmaids, in those days, I will pour out my spirit" (3:1-3).

The Apostles heard from their Lord, Jesus Christ, about the promise of the Spirit, made by his Father. It was above all in his Discourse after the Last Supper that Jesus spoke of the promise and its near realization by the actual coming of the Holy Spirit, the *Paraclete*. I've already cited parts of these verses. Here they are again in full: "If you love me, keep my commandments. And I will ask the Father and he will give you another Advocate to dwell with you forever, the Spirit of truth whom the world cannot receive, because it neither sees him nor knows him. But you shall know him, because he will dwell with you, and be with you" (Jn 14:15-17). "These things I have spoken to you while yet dwelling with you. But the Advocate, the Holy Spirit, whom the Father will send in my name, he will teach all things, and bring to your minds whatever I have said to you" (14:25-26). Lastly:

> *And now I am going to him who sent me, and no one of you asks me, "Where are you going?" But because I have spoken to you these things, sorrow has filled your heart. But I speak the truth to you; it is expedient for you that I depart. For if I do not go, the Advocate will not come to you; but if I go, I will send him to you . . . Many things yet I have to say to you, but you cannot bear them now. But when he, the Spirit of truth, has come, he will teach you all the truth. For he will not speak on his own authority, but whatever he will hear he will speak, and the things that are to come he will declare to you. He will glorify me, because he will receive of what is mine and declare it to you. All things that the Father has are mine. That is why I have said that he will receive of what is mine, and will declare it to you* (16:5-15).

The Holy Spirit, the Spirit of Love, we have tried to contemplate in the Bosom of the Trinity, was not to remain there hidden. Like the Son, he has been sent to the world, but in an invisible and totally spiritual manner, without however leaving the Trinitarian Circle of Love. Promised from the ancient times with the promise of the Messiah, when the "last days," or the Messianic age, inaugurated by the Incarnation of the Word of God, arrived, the Holy Spirit was poured out in fulness first on the Messiah and then on the People of God.

The Gift of the Holy Spirit Before the Glorification of Christ

Before I discuss the outpouring of the Spirit on the Messiah, I will touch briefly on the gift of the Spirit during the times before the coming of the Messiah. We learn from the Old Testament that the Spirit was already at work. Theologians are wont to distinguish a double action of the Spirit: one in which he affects a person from the "outside," in whom he does not yet dwell; and the other in which he acts on a person, *in whom* he dwells.

Though the Holy Spirit "was given to the first man with life," as St. Cyril of Jerusalem says, referring to the passage in Genesis, where it is said that "The Lord God formed man out of the dust of the ground and breathed into his nostrils the breath of life, and man became a living being" (2:7), after the first sin (original sin), the action of the Spirit became "exterior" to human nature. It is in an "exterior" manner that he acts on those who do not yet have the Christian faith. Through the Spirit our Lord may "enlighten every man." Thanks to "exterior" signs—events, encounters, lectures—and "interior" illuminations, the Spirit attracts to Christ the "infidels," without, however, vivifying them with his personal and intimate presence. He is already *with* every man of good will, but he is not yet *in him*. He enters in a person when he believes in Christ, the Savior. Alluding to this double action of the Holy Spirit, St. Augustine wrote: "Before our Lord was glorified by the Resurrection of his flesh, we see many signs of the Holy Spirit, for it certainly was not another Spirit that the Prophets received, who foretold the Advent of Christ. But the Spirit must have been given in a totally different manner then."

Not only the Prophets but also the Judges and the Kings of Israel received the Spirit, or the "Breath of Yahweh."

What the Old Testament calls *Judges* were leaders that the Holy Spirit raised to govern the People of God, to lead them to war, to free them from their enemies. He took possession of them suddenly and clothed them with an extraordinary physical and psychological power. Thus, when the "Spirit of the Lord wrapped Gideon round, one blast of his horn rallied Abiezer's clan behind him" (Jg 6:34), and he was victorious in the camp of Madian. When the Breath (Spirit) of Yahweh took possession of Jephte, he "offered battle to the sons of Ammon, and the Lord gave him the mastery over them" (Jg 11:29-32).

The story of Samson killing a lion is still more typical of the power attributed to the Breath of Yahweh: "So with his father and mother, Samson went to Thamnatha again. And now they had reached the vineyards belonging to the town when of a sudden he met a lion that roared upon him savagely. Thereupon the Spirit of the Lord came down upon Samson, and although he had no weapon, he tore it to pieces as easily as if it had been a kid" (Jg 14:5-6). Later when the men of Juda who feared the Philistines wanted to hand him over to them as a hostage and had tied him with ropes, "the Spirit of the Lord came upon him and his bonds parted and snapped like scorched tow. No weapon had he, but he found a bone lying there, an ass's jaw-bone; took that instead, and killed a thousand men with it" (Jg 15:14-15).

The mission of the Judges was a temporary one, once this mission was accomplished the Spirit departed from them. It was a different affair with the Kings, who succeeded the Judges, for they exercised a permanent function. They were consecrated by a rite: the anointing with oil, which transformed them and obtained for them the active intervention of the Spirit. The prophet Samuel thus will say to Saul: "The Spirit of the Lord shall come upon you . . . and you shall be changed into another man" (1 S 10:6). It is written of David: "Samuel took the horn of oil and anointed him in the midst of his brothers. And the Spirit of the Lord came upon David from that day forward" (1 S 16:13).

When the Kings proved unfaithful to their mission, the Holy Spirit abandoned them, and chose men from the people to transmit the message of God: the Prophets. He endowed them with great power and courage and with knowledge of the ways of God, so they might be able to be his witnesses and to deliver his teachings and warnings. "The Spirit of Yahweh," says Ezechiel, "fell upon me and told me to say: thus says the Lord Yahweh" (Ez 11:5).

The first form of prophetism in Israel consisted for the most part of groups of unruly ecstatics who gave themselves to all sorts of gestures and went into trances and "ravings." An amusing incident in the life of David portrays this group phenomenon. It is found in the First Book of Samuel, and shows the infectious nature of ecstatic prophetism:

> *But David fled and escaped, and came to Samuel in Ramatha, and told him all that Saul had done to him. And he and Samuel went and dwelt in Najoth. And it was told Saul by some, saying: Behold David is in Najoth in Ramatha. So Saul sent officers to take David: and when they saw a company of prophets raving (prophesying), and Samuel presiding over them, the Spirit of the Lord came also upon them, and they likewise began to rave (to prophesy). And when this was told Saul, he sent other messengers; but they also raved (prophesied). And again Saul sent messengers the third time; and they raved (prophesied) also. And Saul being exceedingly angry, went himself to Ramatha, and came as far as the great cistern, which is in Socho, and he asked, and said: "In what place are Samuel and David?" And it was told him: "Behold they are in Najoth in Ramatha." And he went to Najoth in Ramatha. And the Spirit of the Lord came upon him also; and he went on, and raved (prophesied) till he came to Najoth in Ramatha. And he stripped himself also of his garments, and raved (prophesied) with the rest before Samuel, and lay down naked all that day and night (19:18-24).*

It seems hardly necessary to point out that the prophet is not solely nor primarily someone who foretells the future, but, according to the etymology of the word which comes from the Greek *phemi*: one who "speaks for" God, someone who is the instrument, the mouth through which God speaks to men; in short, his spokesman to announce his words, to remind the people of it, and also to foretell the future. But the Spirit touched the Prophets only for the short periods of inspiration and during the carrying out of their mission; and then the Spirit left them.

The Holy Spirit also acted at the beginnings of the New

Testament, on particular persons to whom God had given a part in his redemptive plan. Such was the case of the parents of St. John the Baptist: "And it came to pass, tells St. Luke, "when Elizabeth heard the greeting of Mary, that the babe in her womb leapt. And Elizabeth was filled with the Holy Spirit" (Lk 1:41). A little later on, the Evangelist says: "Zachary . . . was filled with the Holy Spirit and prophesied" (1:67). Such was the case also of John the Baptist himself, of whom it was said: "He shall be great before the Lord; he shall drink no wine or strong drink, and shall be filled with the Holy Spirit even from his mother's womb" (1:15). Such was the case of the old Simeon: "Now, there was in Jerusalem a man named Simeon, and this man was just and devout, looking for the consolation of Israel, and the Holy Spirit was upon him. And it had been revealed to him by the Holy Spirit that he would not see death before he had seen the Christ of the Lord. And he came by inspiration of the Spirit into the Temple" (Lk 2:25-27). Such was the case, finally and principally, of Mary to whom the Angel announced: "The Holy Spirit shall come upon thee and therefore the Holy One to be born shall be called the Son of God" (1:35).

Nevertheless, as I have said earlier, these different outpourings of the Spirit took place now and then and only in favor of certain persons and with measure, in view of a definite mission. Only the power of the Spirit was engaged and not the giving of his Person, except for Jesus and his Mother.

The Outpouring of the Holy Spirit upon Christ

But when the "last days" had arrived, the Holy Spirit was poured forth in a new manner, consisting in the gift of the very Person of the Spirit, in addition to his action. This outpouring was an interior and permanent one. It took place, first of all, upon the Elect of God from the moment of his conception in the womb of Mary, and then after Christ was glorified, upon his people.

The Elect of God, upon whom the Holy Spirit first outpoured himself and who will be the Anointed *par excellence*, is the expected Messiah. Now, the Messiah is Jesus. To the Samaritan woman who said to him: "I know that the Messiah is coming, who is called

Christ," didn't Jesus answer, "I who speak with thee am he"? (Jn 4:25-26).

The Holy Spirit took possession of Jesus from the moment of his conception. If it is said of John the Baptist that he would "be filled with the Holy Spirit even from his mother's womb," all the more must we say that of Christ. In fact, "he was conceived of the Holy Spirit." Therefore, from the moment of his conception, he was filled with the Holy Spirit, with a fullness: "For not by measure does God give him the Spirit," as John the Baptist said of him (Jn 3:34). That is why Jesus is called *Christ*, a Greek word meaning the *Anointed*,—Messiah in Hebrew.

First of all, the Holy Spirit announced the coming of Christ, by the mouth of the Prophets. Through them, the Spirit announced the virginal conception of Jesus: "The Virgin shall be with child and bear a son, and shall name him Emmanuel" (Is 7:14; cf. Mt 1:22-23); *his birth at Bethlehem*: "But you, Bethlehem-Ephratha too small to be among the clans of Juda, from you shall come forth for me one who is to be ruler in Israel, whose origin is from of old, from ancient times" (Mi 5:1; cf. Mt 2:5-6)—*the massacre of the holy Innocents, slain in his place*: "In Rama is heard the sound of moaning, of bitter weeping! Rachel mourns her children, she refuses to be consoled because her children are no more" (Jr 31:15; cf. Mt 2:18); *the flight to Egypt and his return to Nazareth*: "When Israel was a child, I loved him; out of Egypt I called my son" (Ho 11:1; cf. Mt 2:15).

St. Matthew cited all these passages as referring to major events of the life of the Child Jesus. The Evangelist begins the citations with these words: "Now all this came to pass that what was spoken by the Lord through the Prophets might be fulfilled" (1:22). One could cite other passages from the Old Testament relating to the life of Christ. This one for instance, which announces his baptism: "A shoot shall sprout from the stump of Jesse, and from his roots a bud shall blossom. The Spirit of the Lord shall rest upon him: the Spirit of wisdom and understanding, the Spirit of counsel and of strength, the Spirit of knowledge and of fear of the Lord" (Is 11:1-2).

The Holy Spirit traced in advance the essential traits of the Man Jesus, notably in this other prophecy of Isaias (Is 42:1-4) which St. Matthew cited (12:15-21): "Many followed Jesus and he cured them all, and warned them not to make him known; that what was spoken through Isaias the prophet might be fulfilled, who said:

> *Behold, my servant, whom I have chosen,*
> *my beloved in whom my soul is well pleased:*
> *I will put my Spirit upon him,*
> *and will declare justice to the Gentiles,*
> *He will not be contentious or a lover of faction,*
> *none will hear his voice in the streets.*
> *A bruised reed he will not break,*
> *and a smoking wick he will not quench,*
> *Till he will establish justice unfailingly*
> *and in his name will the Gentiles hope.*

The Holy Spirit also traced the fundamental lines of the message of Christ, especially in another passage of Isaias (61:1-2), which St. Luke cites in his Gospel: "Jesus came to Nazareth, where he had been brought up and according to his custom, he entered the synagogue on the Sabbath and stood up to read. And the volume of Isaias the prophet was handed to him. And after he opened the volume, he found the place where it was written:

> *'The Spirit of the Lord is upon me;*
> *because he has anointed me;*
> *He has sent me to bring good news to the poor,*
> *to proclaim to the captives release, to heal*
> *broken hearts, and to give sight to the blind;*
> *To set at liberty the oppressed,*
> *to proclaim the acceptable year of the Lord,*
> *and the day of the Lord's pardon.'*

"And closing the volume, he gave it back to the attendant and sat down. And the eyes of all in the synagogue were gazing on him. But he began to say to them, 'Today this Scripture has been fulfilled in your hearing' " (Lk 4: 16-21).

The Holy Spirit described in advance the Passion of Jesus. Here, for instance, what the Psalmist and Isaias say about the suffering Messiah.

In Psalm 21, we read this most striking and detailed prophecy:

My God, my God, why have you forsaken me,
   far from my prayer, from the words of my cry?
. . . But I am a worm, not a man;
   the scorn of men, despised by the people.
All who see me scoff at me;
   they mock me with parted lips, they wag their heads:
"He relied on the Lord; let him deliver him.

Be not far from me, for I am in distress;
   be near, for I have no one to help me.
Many bullocks surround me;
   the strong bulls of Basan encircle me.
They open their mouths against me
   like ravening and roaring lions.

I am like water poured out;
   all my bones are racked.
My heart has become like wax
   melting away within my bosom.
My throat is dried up like baked clay
   my tongue cleaves to my jaws;
   to the dust of death you have brought me down.

Indeed, many dogs surround me,
   a pack of evildoers closes in upon me;
They have pierced my hands and my feet;
   I can count all my bones.
They look on and gloat over me;
   they divide my garments among them,
   and for my vesture they cast lots.

The prophet Isaias too narrated in advance the suffering and death of
Jesus:

See my Servant . . . so marred was his look beyond that of
man, and his appearance beyond that of mortals . . . Who
would believe what we have heard? To whom has the arm of
the Lord been revealed? He grew up like a sapling before

him, like a shoot from the parched earth; there was in him no stately bearing to make us look at him, no appearance that should attract us to him. He was spurned and avoided by men, a man of suffering, accustomed to infirmity, one of those from whom men hide their faces, spurned, and we held him in low esteem.

Yet it was our infirmities that he bore, our sufferings that he endured, while we thought of him as stricken, as one smitten by God and afflicted. But he was pierced for our offenses, crushed for our sins; upon him was the chastisement that makes us whole, by his stripes we were healed. We had all gone astray like sheep, each following his own way; but the Lord laid upon him the guilt of us all.

Though he was harshly treated, he submitted and opened not his mouth; like a lamb led to the slaughter or a sheep before the shearers, he was silent and opened not his mouth. Oppressed and condemned, he was taken away, and who would have thought any more of his destiny? When he was cut off from the land of the living and smitten for the sin of his people, a grave was assigned him among the wicked and a burial place with evildoers, though he had done no wrong nor spoken any falsehood. But the Lord was pleased to crush him in infirmity.

If he gives his life as an offering for sin, he shall see his descendants in a long life, and the will of the Lord shall be accomplished through him. Because of his afflictions he shall see the light in fulness of days; through his suffering, my Servant shall justify many, and their guilt he shall bear (32:13-15, 53:1-11).

One can say that the Holy Spirit wrote the life of Christ in advance. Our Lord may have read his life as the Messiah in the Old Testament book. Didn't he say to the pilgrims of Emmaus: " 'O foolish ones and slow of hearing to believe in all that the prophets have spoken! Did not the Christ have to suffer the things before entering into his glory?'

And beginning then with Moses and with all the Prophets, he interpreted to them in all the Scriptures the things referring to himself" (Lk 24:25-27). And to the eleven Apostles, reunited with other disciples, Jesus declared: "These are the words which I spoke to you while I was yet with you, that all things must be fulfilled that are written in the Law of Moses and the Prophets and the Psalms concerning me" (24:44).

Under the action of the Spirit the righteous of the Old Testament called on Christ, who was named "the Desired One of all the nations." When the "fullness of time" came, the moment appointed by God for the sending of his Son in the world, it was again the Holy Spirit who brought about the Incarnation in the womb of the Virgin Mary.

It was the Spirit who manifested Jesus to the world, first through the aged man Simeon, as we read in St. Luke:

There was in Jerusalem a man named Simeon, and this man was just and devout, looking for the consolation of Israel, and the Holy Spirit was upon him. It had been revealed to him by the Holy Spirit that he should not see death before he had seen Christ the Lord. And he came by inspiration of the Spirit into the temple. And when his parents brought in the child Jesus, to do according to the custom of the Law, he also received him into his arms and blessed God saying,
"Now thou dost dismiss thy servant, O Lord,
according to thy word, in peace;
Because my eyes have seen thy salvation,
which thou hast prepared before the face of
all people:
A light of revelation to the Gentiles,
and a glory for thy people Israel" (Lk 2:25-32).

The Holy Spirit again revealed Jesus to the world, through the words of John the Baptist. We read in the Gospel of St. John:

John saw Jesus coming to him, and he said, "Behold, the lamb of God, who takes away the sin of the world! This is he of whom I said, 'After me there comes one who has been set above me, because he was before me.' And I did not know

*him. But that he may be known to Israel, for this reason have
I come baptizing with water.'*

*And John bore witness, saying, 'I beheld the Spirit
descending as a dove from heaven, and it abode upon him.
And I did not know him. But he who sent me to baptize with
water said to me, He upon whom thou wilt see the Spirit
descending and abiding upon him, he it is who baptizes with
the Holy Spirit. And I have seen and have borne witness that
this is the Son of God* (Jn 1:29-34).

Before manifesting Jesus through the words of John the Baptist, the
Holy Spirit first pointed out him to the Precursor. But it was not only
to reveal to the Precursor the identity of the Christ that the Holy
Spirit descended on our Lord at his Baptism. It is also because this
descent of the Spirit had a capital role to play at the inauguration of
Jesus' public life and during all his life. Alluding to the Baptism of
Jesus, St. Peter will say to the pagans gathered in the house of the
centurion Cornelius, at Caesarea: "You know what took place
throughout Judea: for he began in Galilee after the baptism preached
by John: how God anointed Jesus of Nazareth with the Holy Spirit
and with power, and went about doing good and healing all who were
in the power of the devil" (Ac 10:37-38).

What do the words, "God anointed Jesus with the Holy Spirit
and with power," signify? The anointing is a mark made with oil; it
means the consecration of a human being for the service of God, who
clothes him with power, symbolized by oil, in view of a determined
mission, as it was the case of priests, prophets and kings in the Old
Testament. The Christ was consecrated by God by an anointing not
of oil but of the Holy Spirit. Jesus was thus clothed with the power of
the Holy Spirit to accomplish the mission confided to him by his
Father. It is to the Spirit that Jesus has his name of "Christ", which
actually means "He who is anointed."

The anointing of the Spirit which Jesus received at his Baptism is
not to be seen as his first anointing. He received that at the moment of
his conception in the womb of Mary. The anointing is sacerdotal:
Jesus is a priest, not as Son of God, but as man united to the divine
nature in the unique person of the Son of God. "There is one God,"
says St. Paul, "and one Mediator between God and men, himself

man, Jesus Christ" (1 Tm 2:5). As Son of God, Jesus is equal to the Father and to the Holy Spirit. Now, the Three Divine Persons, being perfectly equal among themselves, none of them can exercise the role of mediator, or priest, in regard to the other two. As long as he remained in the bosom of his Father, as long as he hadn't become man, the Son of God could not be a priest. It was not suitable for him to humble himself before God the Father to adore and pray to him. The Son of God is a priest only because of his Incarnation. His priesthood is the exclusive prerogative of his human nature—united with the divine nature. It was at the very moment when this union was realized that Jesus was made priest by God, and the One Mediator between God and men. Since it was the Holy Spirit who brought about this union, it was by him that, at the very moment that this union took place, God conferred the anointing to Jesus, that consecrated him a priest. We read in the Letter to the Hebrews: "When God introduced his only-begotten Son in the world, he said: 'O God, thy God, has anointed thee with the oil of gladness above thy fellows' " (Heb 1:5-9).

As for the anointing that Jesus received at his baptism, it was conferred on him, in view of his public life. Through it "the Christ," says Vatican II, "was impelled to begin his ministry." It was an anointing both oral and prophetic, since his mission was going to be precisely a royal and prophetic ministry.

A *royal* anointing, because the Christ had for his mission to bring back men to his Father, from whom they have turned away, to conduct them to their salvation, and into the glory of God. As it is well known, the Latin word *rex*, which means king, comes from *regere*: to conduct, guide and direct. To accomplish this salvation, the Christ had to free men from their sins and death, and from the power of Satan. God therefore anointed this Son with the "Spirit and with power," in order to give him the necessary force to effect this liberation, all the more since all this was to be realized by his death on the Cross.

Also a *prophetic* anointing, because to be accomplished, the mission of Christ also required the preaching of the Word of God, the proclamation of the good tidings of salvation, which he brought on earth; and because, as we know, a prophet is one who speaks in the place and in the name of God. Insofar as he is the eternal Word of

God, Christ is the very Word of God, insofar as he is man, he was anointed with the Holy Spirit to preach the Word of God. Let us recall the prophecy of Isaias, cited by St. Luke, and I have quoted earlier: "The Spirit of the Lord is upon me, because he has anointed me; he has sent me to bring good news to the poor . . . and to proclaim . . . the day of the Lord's pardon." Through the prophetic anointing, the Holy Spirit then invested publicly the Christ with such a power that he will teach "as a man having authority" (Mk 1:22), and will make people say of him, "Never has man spoken as this man" (Jn 7:46).

The descent of the Holy Spirit upon Jesus at his baptism tells yet another aspect of his role in the mission of the Messiah. "Immediately on coming up from the water he saw the heavens opened and the Spirit, as a dove, descending and remaining upon him. And there came a voice from the heavens, 'Thou art my beloved Son, in thee I am well pleased' " (Mk 1:10-11).

This passage of St. Mark expresses first the authenticity of the mission of Jesus by God. Now, on the one hand, by testifying publicly his paternal love of Jesus. God verifies the divine filiation of Jesus, and announces the adoptive filiation of believers—which will be a participation in Jesus' filiation, and thus the gift of the Spirit. On the other hand, this witness is given by the sending of the Holy Spirit upon him. The Spirit is consequently the living witness of the love of the Father for the Christ, and therefore the authentication of his mission. The Spirit is the very love that the Father has for Jesus, and it would seem that this is one reason why the Spirit descended upon Jesus under the form of a dove.

The biblical dove also symbolizes love. In the Song of Songs, the lover calls the beloved, "My dove." In the Genesis account of the creation of the world, the dove appears implicitly as the symbol of the Holy Spirit. "In the beginning God created the heavens and the earth; the earth was waste and void: darkness covered the abyss, and the Spirit of God was stirring above the waters" (Gn 1:1). From Scripture we learn that God created the universe to express through it his love for man. The universe is a song of love, a word of the Creator to communicate his love: a word of love, material echo of the Word of Love the Father utters in the Trinity; a created word, image of the uncreated Word, through which God manifests to man his glory, i.e., makes him know his love. It was fitting that the Holy Spirit "stirred" above the primordial waters, as God created the universe: the visible sign of his uncreated Love.

The biblical dove fittingly symbolizes the Spirit of Love, because it also symbolizes the fruit of God's love: the messianic Community, the Church: the "New Israel."

In commenting on the baptism of Jesus, Fr. Lagrange writes: "Just as the Holy Spirit hovered over the primordial waters like a dove, so the Spirit descends in the form of a dove before Jesus has left the waters of the Jordan: the Holy Spirit will act the same way upon the waters to give them a supernatural power." Thus, he adds, "at the very moment when Jesus submits himself to the baptism of water, he transforms it into baptism of the Holy Spirit, who will give birth to the messianic community." The dove, at the baptism of Jesus, designates essentially regenerated Israel, "the perfect community in the era of grace," as A. Feuillet puts it—realized by the sudden eruption of the Holy Spirit.

Fr. A.M. Henry, O.P., in his book, *The Holy Spirit* (Hawthorne Books, 1960 pp. 46-7), has written a most vivid page on the significance of the biblical dove:

> Indeed, for Osee, the dove is the people of Israel returning from exile, purified at last: "Fluttering like a sparrow or dove from Egypt, from the Assyrian country, and in their own home, the Lord says, I will give them rest" (Ho 11:11; cf. 7:11). For the psalmist too, the dove is the people loved by God: "Wilt thou throw to wild beasts, thy dove?" (Ps 73:19).

> It is the people which "as a dove with silvered wings" settles in Canaan (Ps 67:14). But for the Jews in the time of Christ it is especially the people of Israel, referred to as a dove in the Song of Songs. The phrase: "my dove, my perfect one" (Sg 2:14; 5:2; 6:9 and also 1:15; 4:1; 5:12) describes "the spouse of Yahweh in the state which is to be its own once the covenant is restored, and it refers to the longing for the new Exodus announced by the prophets." (Feuillet)

> Thus John, who baptized Jesus and saw the dove, symbol of

the spouse, can cry out: "The bride is for the bridegroom" (Jn 3:29). He adds that "the bridegroom's friend who stands by and listens to him, rejoices too, rejoices at hearing the bridegroom's voice; and this joy is mine in all measure." These words bring to mind also the cry of joy from the spouse in the Song of Songs when she hears "the voice of her true love" (2:8, 10, 14; 5:2). All that John the Baptist discovers about Jesus, he discovers during the baptismal scene. It is there that he recognizes God's Chosen One (Jn 1:34, the Lamb of God (1:29), the Spouse, the substitute for Israel, the messianic king.

The Liturgy made the baptism of Jesus the feast of his wedding with the Church, and in a most beautiful antiphon for the feast of the Epiphany sings: "Today, the Church has been united to the heavenly spouse, for Christ has washed her sins in the Jordan. The Magi hasten with gifts to the royal nuptials and the water, changed into wine, rejoices the wedding-guests, Alleluia."

The story of the baptism of Christ does not tell us only of the role of the Spirit in the authentication by God of the mission of Jesus. It also shows the dominant role the Spirit would play during his mission. He did not descend upon Christ only to inaugurate his apostolic work. In fact, St. Luke writes that: "Jesus, full of the Holy Spirit, returned from the Jordan, and was led by the Spirit into the desert" (4:1); that he "returned in the power of the Spirit into Galilee" (4:14); that "God anointed Jesus of Nazareth with the Holy Spirit and with power, and he went about doing good and healing all" (Ac 10:38). Jesus himself declared that it was by the Holy Spirit that he "cast out devils" (Mt 12:28). It was the Holy Spirit who inspired Jesus' prayer, as we learn from one occasion, narrated by St. Luke: "In that very hour Jesus rejoiced in the Holy Spirit and said, 'I praise thee, Father, Lord of heaven and earth, that thou didst hide these things from the wise and prudent, and didst reveal to little ones" (10:21). All the more we should think that it was on the impulse of the Spirit that Jesus celebrated the Last Supper, where he effected the Eucharist, the perfect prayer of thanksgiving: the total gift of himself. Finally, "it was through the Holy Spirit," writes the author of Hebrews, "that Christ offered himself unblemished unto God" (9:14).

In all things and always Christ was moved by the Holy Spirit; in other words by *Love*. And it is thus that the Spirit made of the life of Jesus, of the message and of his work, a witness of the love of God for man. Rather, the Holy Spirit himself accomplished, in Christ and through Christ, the gracious divine plan of redemption, that the Father confined to his Son: to make possible for man to share the love with which the Father loves his Son, and which is the Holy Spirit himself. As St. Paul writes: "The love of God is poured forth in our hearts by the Holy Spirit who has been given to us" (Rm 5:5).

CHAPTER FOUR

The Holy Spirit in the Mysteries of the Incarnation and of the Redemption

The primordial role played by the Holy Spirit in the life of Christ has shown to us the deep meaning of the sending of the Son of God in the world. God wishes to declare and to give his love to man. The God-Man came in the world to reveal the Father. "No one," says St. John, "has at any time seen God. The only-begotten Son, who is in the bosom of the Father, he has revealed him" (1:18). Jesus has revealed the Father through what he did, said, and above all, wt he is: "He who sees me sees also the Father" (Jn 14:9).

However, the ultimate goal of the redemptive Incarnation was not only to reveal the Father, but also to tell men that the Father loves them as sons, and to communicate his love. The role of the Holy Spirit has been precisely to outpour in man's hearts, by Jesus Christ and in Jesus Christ, the love of the Father. Now, this role of the Spirit began from the moment the Son of God was conceived in the bosom of Mary; and continued in the mystery of his death and Resurrection, to reach completion in his Ascension. The mystery of the Incarnation and the mystery of the Redemption, which includes the death of Jesus, his Resurrection and Ascension, are effectively the work of the Holy Spirit.

The Holy Spirit in the Mystery of the Incarnation

In the eternal *Today* of the Godhead, the Three divine Persons formed a gracious plan, the end of which was their sharing their Life and Love with free creatures. From this plan flows human history as well as the history of redemptive salvation. St. Paul wrote several very beautiful summaries of the divine plan. For instance, in Ephesians:

> *Blessed be the God and Father of our Lord Jesus Christ, who has blessed us with every spiritual blessing on high in Christ. Even as he chose us in him before the foundation of the world, that we should be holy and without blemish in his sight in love. He predestined us to be adopted through Jesus Christ as his sons, according to his gracious plans, for the praise of the glory of his love, with which he has favored us in his beloved Son.*

> *In him we have redemption through his blood, the remission of sins, according to the riches of his grace. This love has abounded beyond measure in us in all wisdom and prudence, so that he may make known the mystery of his will according to his good pleasure. And this his good pleasure he planned in him to be accomplished in the fullness of the times: to re-establish all things in Christ, both those in the heavens and those on the earth (1:3-10).*

Later in this same Letter, St. Paul writes:

> *Yes, to me, the very least of all saints, there was given this grace, to announce among the Gentiles the good tidings of the unfathomable riches of Christ, and to enlighten all men as to what is the plan of the mystery which has been hidden from eternity in God, who created all things; in order that through the Church there be made known . . . the manifold wisdom of God according to the eternal plan which he accomplished in Christ Jesus our Lord. In him we have assurance and confident access through faith in him (3:8-12).*

St. Peter also stresses the divine plan, which was formed in the bosom of God. He writes: "You were redeemed . . . with the precious blood of Christ, as of a lamb without blemish and without spot. Foreknown, indeed, before the foundation of the world, he has been manifested in the last times for your sake. Through him you are believers in God who raised him up from the dead and gave him glory" (1 P 1:18-21).

To the Galatians St. Paul wrote on our adoption as sons: "When the fullness of time came, God sent his Son, born, of a woman, born under the Law, that he might redeem those who were under the Law, that we might receive the adoption of sons" (Gal 4:4-5). The same declaration from St. John: "Behold what manner of love the Father has given to us, that we should be called children of God, and such we are" (1 Jn 3:1).

This loving design was determined by the Three divine Persons together. In the dialogue where, so to say, they planned in their eternal today, the Father decides to send his Son: "God so loved the world that he gave his only begotten Son" (Jn 3:16). The Son decides to take up the human condition: "Sacrifice and oblation thou wouldst not, but a body thou hast fitted to me . . . Then said I, "Behold, I come—in the head of the book it is written of me—to do thy will, O God" (Heb 10:5-7). The Son resolves to "empty" himself, to "appear in the form of man" to "humble himself," to "become obedient to death, even to death on the cross" (Ph 2:5-8). Now, this decision, the Father and the Son took under the inspiration of the common Spirit of Love, by which he gives his consent and engages himself to sustain and animate the redemptive work of the Son (Cf. Heb 9:14): "Christ, who through the Holy Spirit, offered himself unblemished unto God."

"When the fullness of time came," St. Paul wrote, "God sent his Son, born of a woman." It was fitting that *Mary* who was chosen to collaborate in the mystery of the Incarnation, be prepared in her soul and body. Now, as a liturgical prayer has it, it is with the cooperation of the Holy Spirit that God prepared the body and soul of the Virgin Mary so that she merited to become a worthy abode for his Son.

"Mary was used by God not merely in a passive way, but as cooperating in the work of human salvation through her faith and obedience" (*Lumen Gentium:* No. 56). Mary could have perhaps conceived miraculously her infant without God first asking for the adhesion of her faith, or the consent of her free will. Such was not the way chosen by God, for such is not the way of love. Love does not impose itself; it offers itself. That is the way of the Holy Spirit. Being Love in Person, in his dealings with man, he waits for his free cooperation. Far from dispensing with human freedom or forcing it, he respects and favors it in such a way that the consent of love may be more total and solid. Thus he respected fully the freedom of Mary the day when the angel Gabriel announced to her the design of God and asked for her cooperation. The dialogue of Mary with the divine messenger shows that she believed in the angel's words and gave her full consent freely.

Confronted by the divine proposal, Mary remained fully free. The proof of this is seen in the question she asked of the angel about her virginity: "How shall this happen, since I do not know man?" It is well known that the verb "to know" in the biblical expressions, "to know a man," or "to know a woman," means to unite sexually with someone. Mary, in other words, said: "I'm a virgin." Mary had resolved to remain a virgin. She had understood that what was asked of her was to become a mother. How shall this happen; Mary does not see how to reconcile this motherhood with her virginity. She knows that she is not a young girl any more and she knows that she can give birth to a child, and she knows what is here involved. She also knows that she does not belong to any man, and she says so, straight to the point.

Did she understand that she would conceive at that instant, and surprised said, "How is this possible since I have not known any man?" If this was what she meant to say, St. Luke should have made it clear, and should have done so by putting the verb in the past tense. To the question of Mary, understood in this sense, it would have been sufficient for the angel to answer: "What is not yet done, will be done." The *present* in Mary's answer does not refer to the *past*. On the contrary, it can be maintained that it referred to the *future*. In Hebrew, and in Arabic too, the present tense can denote a "continued present," and can be rendered, either by a present or by a future.

Mary meant to say: "I do not know, nor will I know any man." That is why she is unable to reconcile the announced maternity with the promise of virginity that she has made. With her virginity is not only the state of her young age; it is, for now and the future, the resolve to belong totally to God. Consequently, the only satisfying meaning that one can see in the answer of Mary is her resolve to remain a virgin. Moreover, one would be unable to understand otherwise the fact that the angel Gabriel received her question favorably, while he punished Zachary for his.

The question put by Zachary to the same angel Gabriel, who announced to him the conception humanly impossible of a son, was found reprehensible, and Zachary was struck with dumbness. That of Mary, on the contrary, was received favorably by the divine messenger, who hastened to give to the prudent Virgin all the explanations she wished. Why this difference, if not because the question of Zachary proceeded from a doubt? He did not believe in the words of the angel. "How shall I know this? For I am an old man and my wife is advanced in years" (Lk 1:18).

Mary believed the message of the angel. St. Elizabeth, her cousin will congratulate her later, saying to her: "Blessed is she who has believed, because the things promised her by the Lord shall be accomplished" (Lk 1:43). Mary's question proceeded from her firm resolve to remain a virgin at all cost. She needed to have the assurance that she would conceive though remaining a virgin. There was no irreverence in Mary's conduct. She only wished to pose one condition, before giving her answer. She will accept the divine proposal provided she is assured that her vow of virginity will be completely respected. On his part, the angel understood Mary, and to give her the assurance she desired, told her that she would conceive not by the cooperation of a man, but by the power of the Holy Spirit.

Mary's remark, "I do not know man," proves that she was free. Being free Mary could refuse the proposal of the divine messenger. Her refusal could even have had another motive than her firm decision to remain a virgin. The motive could have been to avoid the intense suffering that the prophets had foretold for the Messiah, which she would share as his mother, were she to accept. To agree to be the mother of the Messiah was to accept to be the mother of the "Man of Sorrows," and to drink the chalice that he had to drink— something that even Christ himself will hesitate at one point: Jesus, kneeling down, began to pray, saying, "Father, if thou art willing, remove this cup from me; yet not my will but thine be done" (Lk 22:41-43).

To refuse would have meant to disobey God, to prefer herself to him, to declare (like Adam and Eve) her independence towards him.

It would have meant to thwart the realization of his redemptive plan, at least to its realization by the means chosen by him. Could Mary sin thus? Yes, for though she was full of grace from the first instant of her existence, Mary, like Eve, was not confirmed in grace from the first instant of her existence. Mary, was not confirmed in grace from that instant. Her free will was definitely fixed in the good only after she had cnceived the Word of God. Till then, Mary, wholly immaculate and innocent as she was, had a certain power to sin, only a certain power though, for she did not have the propensity to evil, the consequence of original sin. There was very little risk, however, that Mary would sin.

First she was exempt from original sin and was sanctified from the very moment of her conception. God loved Mary from all eternity with a love of predilection, having chosen her to be the mother of his Son made man, and consequently, the mother of Christ's mystical Body. In view of the eminent role to which he had predestined her, and because of the merits of his Son, God enveloped her with his Spirit of Love—who gave her, from the moment of her conception, a fullness of grace, which conferred upon her a spotless purity and fullness of love.

Her immaculate conception, her fullness of grace, predisposed Mary to believe the message of the angel and readily to accept the divine request. Indeed, moved mightily by the Holy Spirit, her whole being stretched toward the accomplishment of the promise made by God in favor of Abraham and his posterity, as she later sang in her *Magnificat:* "God the Savior has given help to Israel, his servant, mindful of his mercy—even as he spoke to our fathers—to Abraham and to his posterity forever" (Lk 1:54-55).

Mary belonged to that group of just and devout Jews, the "poor and humble servants and handmaidens of the Lord," who, according to St. Luke, were waiting for the redemption of Israel, such as Zachary, the aged Simeon, and Anna the prophetess. Like them, and more than they, she expected with her most ardent desires the coming of the Messiah, who "would save his people from their sins" (Mt 1:21). In her heart flowed and found echo the prayers and wishes of all the reighteous of the Old Testament.

Animated thus by the Holy Spirit, source of all faith and love, Mary freely believed the message of the angel; and no sooner had

Gabriel assured her about her virginity, by telling her that the conception would take place through the action of the Holy Spirit, she accepted, saying, "Behold the handmaid of the Lord; be it done to me according to thy word" (Lk 1:38).

The story of the Annunciation insists far too much on the decision of Mary to remain a virgin for us to fail to see in this resolve a very close relation between her virginity and the miraculous conception that the Holy Spirit was to bring about. The explanation of the angel about the intervention of the Holy Spirit and in answer to Mary's question about her virginity, enlightens us in this connection. The angel Gabriel said to Mary: "The Holy Spirit shall come upon thee and the power of the Most High shall overshadow thee, and therefore the Holy One to be born shall be called the Son of God" (Lk 1:35).

If the Incarnation of the Son of God was brought about through a virginal conception, the reason is not at all that the carnal (or sexual) union is tainted with sin, nor that it is of doubtful moral value. It was fitting that it be brought about this way for several other different reasons.

It was fitting that God the Father not abdicate his Paternity, nor share with another his title of father with regard to him who is his unique Son by nature.

It was fitting for Christ, in the mystery of the hypostatic union, not to have a "carnal" father. By the hypostatic union, Jesus Christ has *two natures,* the divine and the human, but he is *one person,* the Second Person of the Trinity. Now, it is difficult to conceive that the same person could have two fathers, and that would happen to Christ, true Son of God, if he had a father according to the flesh.

It was fitting that the temporal conception of the Word in the womb of Mary be in accord with his eternal generation in the Bosom of the Father, in order that it might be proved that the body of Christ is the body of the Word of God himself. Now, the eternal birth of the Son is the work of the Father *only:* a totally "spiritual" generation. So it had to be for the Word's temporal birth: he was born of the pure womb of the Virgin, showing by that that he was really the Word. The temporal birth of the Word took place by the power of the Holy Spirit: it is the work of love. The Holy Spirit was not alone in the work of the Incarnation of the Word. As an *active* not *passive* operation the Incarnation, like all actions of God accomplished "outside" the Godhead, is the common work of the Three divine Persons. Nevertheless, the active Incarnation is in a special manner, work of the Holy Spirit, since it is a work of love. As he is the bond of Love between the Father and the Son, it belonged to him to unite the divine nature with the human nature in Christ Jesus. Thus Christ is the fruit of love and the gift of God. "God has so loved the world that he gave his only-begotten Son."

It was fitting that Christ be born of a virgin in view of the end of the Incarnation, which is to give man "the power of becoming sons of God," "to be born not of blood, nor of the will of the flesh, nor the will of man, but of God" (Jn 1:12-13), i.e., by the very power of God, hence by a *spiritual birth:* "to be born again of water and the Spirit" (Jn 3-6). Contrary to a human birth, which takes place through a sexual (carnal) act, and from this fact "is weighed down by the flesh and is subjected to the violence of passion," the birth of Christ through the Holy Spirit was a wholly spiritual birth. Though it was brought about in the flesh: "The Word was made flesh," the act which produced it was purely spiritual. The birth becomes a "mystery of a love which is nothing but love, and which makes no concession to sensual egoism." The birth of Christ had to be virginal in order to be the model of our own spiritual rebirth, the work of the Spirit, which will be a birth brought about exclusively by divine love.

It was fitting that Christ be conceived virginally of the Holy Spirit, because the child that would be born of Mary "will be holy," as the angel said to her. The Holy Spirit brings about the sanctification of the soul and body of Jesus from the instant of his conception. While human conception gives birth to infants deprived of sanctifying grace, the Virgin Mary excepted, the conception by the Holy Spirit can produce only an infant of total holiness. That is why, the rebirth of men of "the water and Spirit" makes them saints, of the very holiness of the Holy Spirit.

Finally, it was fitting that the woman, in whom the Son of God was to become man, be and remain a virgin, because it was by uniting to her, that by her and in her, God was going to unite himself to the whole of humanity, in the person of his Son. In the Old Testament, in order to make his chosen people understand the covenant of love that he had contracted with them, God compared it to a *marriage*. For instance, in Isaias we read:

> *The Lord calls you back, like a wife forsaken and grieved in spirit, a wife married in youth and then cast off, says your God. For a brief moment I abandoned you, but with great tenderness I will take you back. In an outburst of wrath, for a moment I hid my face from you; but with enduring love I take pity on you, says the Lord, your redeemer* (Is 54:6-8).

And in Osee:

> *On that day, says the Lord, you shall call me "My husband," and never again "My baal." Then will I remove from her mouth the name of the Baals, so that they shall be no longer invoked. I will make a covenant for them on that day, with the beasts of the field. . . Bow and sword and war I will destroy from the land, and I will let them take their rest in security* (Ho 2:18-20).

Jesus Christ, the Messiah, brought about this "marriage," and with the whole of humanity He presented himself as the Bridegroom. Defending his disciples from the criticism of the Pharisees, Jesus said to them: "Can you make the wedding guests fast as long as the bridegroom is with them? But the days will come—and when the bridegroom shall be taken away from them, then they will fast in those days" (Lk 6:34-35). The divine wedding that the Prophets foretold, that the Psalms sang and the Song of Songs, found its realization in the mystery of Christ and the Church. Through his Incarnation, the Word of God has espoused in the womb of the Virgin Mary a determined, singular human nature, and formed with it Jesus Christ. The Word of God united thus to a singular human nature, in the unity of the person of Christ, in order to unite to himself the whole of saved humanity: to make of redeemed humanity a Spouse forever, a Spouse born from Christ's open side and purified in his divine blood.

The Bridegroom, announced and sung in the Old Testament, is

then Christ, since he is the Word of God, the Second Person of the Trinity; it is this Person that has espoused human nature, by becoming flesh in the womb of Mary, thanks to her acceptance of the divine plan. The Bride, is redeemed humanity, the Church, that is to say, all mankind because all belong to it, actually or potentially, for as St. Paul says, "God wishes all men to be saved" (1 Tm 2:4-6). This mystical marriage takes place however actually with those who believe in Christ. Of these, St. Paul wrote: "I have betrothed you to one spouse that I might present you a chaste virgin to Christ" (2 Cor 11:2).

The Fathers of the Church spoke often about this doctrine. St. Augustine said: "The nuptial bed of the Bridegroom is the womb of the Virgin, since in it were united the Bridegroom and the Bride: the Bridegroom, i.e., the Word, the Bride, i.e., human flesh, as it is written: "They shall be two in one flesh . . . To this flesh the Church will be joined, and will form the Total Christ, the head and the body" (*Tract on the Epistle of St. John*). St. Gregory the Great wrote: "God the Father brought about the wedding of his only-begotten Son, when he united him to human nature in the virginal womb of Mary, when he willed that his Son, God before the time, become man at the end of time. . . More confidently, we can say that the King celebrates the nuptials of his Son when he gives the Church for his companion, in the mystery of the Incarnation" (Hom. 38 in Evang.).

Of this humanity, and more particularly of this Church that the Word wanted to wed Mary was to be the first and the most eminent member. The word, first of all, became her bridegroom, when she consented, and in her womb he married the Church, or redeemed humanity. That is why God had need of a virginal heart that was capable to receive fully his love, with which he could bring about the matrimonial covenant, announced in the Old Testament, and about to be realized through the Incarnation of his Son.

For all these reasons, it was as a virgin that Mary was invited to cooperate in this Incarnation. Her preparation to this virginal collaboration was the work of the Holy Spirit. He inspired her, who was going to be a spouse of the Word and the mother of Christ, to reserve her heart for God. It was fitting that this role be attributed to the Holy Trinity, who is Love personified and the bond of love of the Father and the Son. It is the Spirit who inspired Mary to consecrate herself to God through her virginity, and who strengthened her in this resolve.

In view of her cooperation in the mystery of the Incarnation, Mary has been "fashioned by the Holy Spirit" (*Lumen Gentium. No. 56).* From the beginning up to the end of her existence, she was entirely docile, body and soul, to the Spirit of Love.

The Holy Spirit In The Mystery of The Redemption

Like the Incarnation, Redemption too is the work of divine love, and hence of the Holy Spirit: Redemption, namely, the redeeming act of Christ, which comprises his death on the Cross, his Resurrection and his Ascension to the heavens. "God, who is rich in mercy," writes St. Paul to the Ephesians, "by reason of his great love wherewith he has loved us even when we were dead by reason of our sins, brought us to life together with Christ—by grace you have been saved—and raised us up together, and seated us together in heaven in Jesus Christ" (2:4-6).

Work of divine love as it is, our Redemption was to be accomplished, as was the Incarnation, under the inspiration and the action of the Holy Spirit. And indeed it was in all three phases, that St. Paul enumerated above.

As concerns the *crucifixion,* a verse of Hebrews, which I have already cited, says that Christ "through the Holy Spirit offered himself unblemished unto God." It was under the mighty impulse of the Spirit of love that Christ suffered his passion and shed his blood. Indeed, it is not the sufferings of Christ which redeems the world, it is his *obedience* to his Father, or more exactly, it is his *love* for his Father, a love which he expressed through his sufferings and his ignominious death on the Cross. "It is necessary," Jesus said to his Apostles during the Last Supper, "that the world know that I love the Father, and that I do as the Father has commanded me" (Jn 14:31). It is this love that made St. John of the Cross say: "I gaze at your Cross, O Christ, and I read in it the song of your love."

The Cross is the song of the love of Christ for his Father, but also of his love for men, whom he has made his friends and brothers. Didn't he say: "Greater love than this no one has, that one lay down his life for his friends?" (Jn 15:3). And St. John will write: "In this we have come to know his love, that he laid down his life for us" (1 Jn 3:16).

Since the Holy Spirit is the Spirit of Love, we should not be surprised to learn that he played also a primordial role in the sacrificial act of Christ, where is expressed the greatest love. From the side of Christ, pierced on the Cross—to which he alluded when he spoke of the living waters flowing from within him—it was the Holy Spirit who came forth under the symbol of living waters. Christ loves man with a human love, but this human love is the expression of divine love. Though the act of the human will by which he loves us, as man, differs from the act of the divine will by which he loves us, as the Son of God, yet the love expressed by the one and the other of the two wills are one and the same love, by virtue of the unicity of the person of Jesus Christ: the Word of God made man. Consequently, the love with which Christ loves us with his heart of flesh is the same love with which the Father loves us. Through Christ's human love then the love of the Father and the Son is revealed and given, and this love is the Holy Spirit, who is the mutual love of the Father and the Son and becomes through Christ, the Gift of the one and the other to humanity. "The love of God is poured forth in our hearts by the Holy Spirit who has been given to us," (Rm 5:5). The Spirit has intervened in a most special way in the redeeming sacrifice of Christ on the Cross.

This intervention was shown by the joy which Christ felt on the vigil of his death and which is one of the characteristic notes of the Holy Spirit: the eternal joy of the Father and the Son. "These things I have spoken to you that my joy may be in you, and that your joy may be full" (Jn 15:1). And a little later, speaking of his Father, he said: "But now, I am coming to thee, and these things I speak in the world, in order that they may have my joy and be made full in themselves" (8:11).

The Holy Spirit also played a primary role in the Resurrection of Christ, as he did in his crucifixion. St. Paul, indeed, says that the Spirit was the instrumental cause of the Resurrection. He writes thus to the Romans: "If the Spirit of him who raised Jesus from the dead dwells in you, then he who raised Jesus Christ from the dead will also bring to life your mortal bodies beacuse of his Spirit who dwells in you" (8:11).

To speak properly, it is God the Father who is the author of the Resurrection, ours as well as that of Christ. However, it is the product of the power of God. That is why it is attributed to him who is the personal power of God: the Holy Spirit. God works, through the power of his Spirit, in giving to mortal flesh a participation of the spirituality and the immortality of this Spirit.

It is difficult for us to image the reality of the risen body of the Lord. As we read in the New Testament, Our Lord, when he arose from the dead, did not cast off his humanity. It was he, in flesh and blood, and not a spirit, that the disciples saw, heard and touched. St. Luke narrates:

> *Jesus stood in their midst, and said to them, "Peace be to you! It is I, do not be afraid." But they were startled and panic stricken, and thought they saw a spirit. And he said to them, "Why are you disturbed, and why do doubts arise in your hearts? See my hands and feet, that it is I myself. Feel me and see; for a spirit does not have flesh and bones, as you see I have." And having said this, he showed them his hands and his feet. But as they still disbelieved and marvelled for joy, he said, "Have you anything here to eat?" And they offered him a piece of broiled fish and a honeycomb. And when he had eaten in their presence, he took what remained and gave it to them* (Lk 24:36-43).

The humanity of Jesus remains, is visible, sensible and tangible. It keeps through its scars the traces of his passion and death. Yet it is not the same. After his Resurrection, Our Lord leads a new life: he appears, disappears, goes from one place to another faster than light, as a flash of lightning, goes through closed doors. His humanity is transformed, and this transfiguration affects both his soul and his body. As St. Paul puts it, the body of the risen Lord has ceased to be *natural*; it has been absorbed by the Spirit and *spiritualized.*

Let us examine more closely St. Paul's text, just alluded above. It will permit us to understand a little better the nature of the resurrected body of Christ, and the capital role of the Holy Spirit in the Lord's Resurrection and Ascension.

Discussing the doctrine of the resurrection from the dead, St.

Paul says of the body that "what is sown a natural body rises as a spiritual body." And he goes on to say:

> *If there is a natural body, there is also a spiritual body. So also it is written, "The first man, Adam, became a living soul"; the last Adam became a life-giving spirit. But it is not the spiritual that comes first, but the psychical, and then the spiritual. The first man was of the earth, earthy; the second man is from heaven, heavenly. As was the earthy man, such also are earthy; and as is the heavenly man, such also are the heavenly. Therefore, even as we have borne the likeness of the earthy, let us bear also the likeness of the heavenly. Now this I say, brethren, that flesh and blood can obtain no part in the kingdom of God, neither shall corruption have any part in incorruption* (1 Cor 15:44-50).

Wanting to establish the possibility of the glorious resurrection, St. Paul, as we see, opposes two bodies, a body which he calls *natural* and another which he calls *spiritual.*

The natural (psychical) body is that which comes from Adam; it is the *flesh,* which animates only our physiological life: the animal soul, in Greek, the *psyche,* the vital principle of the animal soul, the vital principle we have in common with the animals, the breath of life that God breathed "in the nostrils of Adam," as the Old Testament puts it in its imaginative language, and thanks to which man becomes a living soul, namely, precisely a being living a *natural life.*

The spiritual body is that which is vivified by the *Pneuma,* i.e., by the Holy Spirit, who is the vivifying breath of divine love. From St. Paul's text, we learn that the body of Christ, after having been a natural (psychical) body during his terrestrial existence, became a spiritual body after his Resurrection. Son of Adam, Christ was fashioned according to the image of the common ancestor; he too carried the image of the terrestrial man; to him the words are to be applied: It is not the spiritual body which was first, but the natural (psychical).

In becoming man, the Word of God took up "the likeness of sinful flesh," according the expression of St. Paul (Rm 8:3); that is to say, "a body of flesh and blood," like ours, infirm, feeble and mortal.

After his Resurrection, Christ became "a vivifying spirit." This does not mean only that Christ became the principle of the spiritual and immortal life. It also means that Our Lord began to exist in a spiritual body. From then on, the vital principle of Christ is no longer an animal soul, corruptible and mortal, the *psyche;* he became spiritual, by participating in the Holy Spirit, who transformed in *pneuma,* in the breath of incorruptible and immortal life. The Holy Spirit communicates his own vitality to the corporal humanity of Jesus and transforms it, by printing his form: he spiritualizes it. The body of Christ, being re-united with his soul, on the morning of the Resurrection, though it remained corporal, was penetrated by the Spirit of God, who possessed thenceforth this soul without being any longer constricted by its carnal envelope. It was spiritualized by him, vivified, with an incorruptible and immortal life. It ceased to be terrestrial and became heavenly: it ceased to be a wretched body and became a glorious body, now spiritual, completely penetrated by him, whom St. Peter calls, "the Spirit of glory."

We see by the event itself what role the Holy Spirit played in the Ascension of the Lord. "Flesh and blood," as St. Paul says, "can obtain no part in the kingdom of God, neither shall corruption have any part in incorruption," namely, that the human body subject to the laws of matter, to corruption and to death, cannot enter into the bosom of God, who being spiritual and incorruptible cannot admit in him anything of matter, yet less of mortal. That is why St. Paul concludes: "This corruptible body must put on incorruption and this mortal body must put on immortality." Having a "body of flesh and blood," or a "natural body," Christ needed, in order to enter into the glory of his Father, to be freed from the corruptible and mortal body and to have a "spiritual body," a glorified body. On the vigil of his death Jesus said to his apostles: "If you loved me, you would indeed rejoice that I am going to the Father" (Jn 14:28). It was then death which glorified his body, that gave his body the qualities— incorruptibility and immortality—which St. Paul attributes to the body after the resurrection. It was in death that Christ was "swallowed up in victory," the victory of the Resurrection.

Thus transfigured by the Holy Spirit, from a being of flesh and blood, into an incorruptible and immortal being, though remaining corporal, Our Lord could penetrate into the bosom of God. In fact, the Epistle to the Hebrews declares, in more than one place that the event took place that way. "Has taken his seat at the right hand of the Majesty on high" (Heb 1:3)"; He has taken his seat forever at the right hand of God; (10:12) "Jesus has not entered into a Holies made by hands, a mere copy of the true, but into heaven itself, to appear before the face of God on our behalf" (9:24). All these expressions signify an intimate communion with God.

The entrance into the heavens, this sitting at the right hand of God is called, as we will know, the Ascension. It too was the work of the Holy Spirit: "After he had given commandments to the apostles he had chosen, Jesus was taken up to the heavens through the Holy Spirit" (Ac: 1-2).

The transformation brought about by the Spirit in our Lord affected not only his body but also, and first of all, his soul. Before the Resurrection of his body, the soul of Jesus, immediately after his death, was invaded by the Holy Spirit. Through his entrance into glory, the opposition was abolished between his carnal life and his life according to the Spirit; between the form of the slave he had taken up for love of us and his divine condition as Son of God. Christ was invaded by the Holy Spirit and his divine filiation was perfected by his entrance into the bosom of the Father. It is true that Jesus was the Son of God from the first instant of his conception in the bosom of Mary, but it is thanks to his glorification that his divine filiation has reached its full flowering and glory. St. Paul says of him: "Born according to the flesh of the offspring of David, he was established in his power of Son of God, in keeping with the Spirit of holiness, by the resurrection from the dead" (Rm 1:3-4). "During the days of his flesh," Christ had hidden the divine glory, due to him as Son of God. The flesh was like an opaque veil, which hid the divine light and beauty and impeded its radiance, except on the day of the Transfiguration on the sacred Mountain of Thabor. Death took away the veil; and the gracious splendor of divine life spread on Christ, first on his soul. It was in the first glorious state that, before his Resurrection, our Lord "put to death in the flesh, but brought to life in the Spirit, went to preach to those spirits who were in prison" (1 P 3:18-21), to free the souls of the deceased, by his "descent into hell." The Resurrection realized in his body what the Holy Spirit had effected in his soul.

CHAPTER FIVE

The Holy Spirit, Promise of the Father and the Son Realized

The work of the Holy Spirit in the mystery of the Redemption was not only to impel Christ to Calvary, to raise him from the dead and to make him enter into the glory of his Father. In addiion to these events, the Holy Spirit brought about the realization of the promise of the Father and the Son of his own sending upon the people of God. The gift of the Holy Spirit is the goal of God's plan, the purpose towards which he had ordered everything.

According to the divine plan, the sending of the Spirit was to take place after the glorification of Christ. St. John writes: "On the last, the great day of the feast (of Tabernacles), Jesus stood and cried out, saying, "If anyone thirst, let him come to me and drink, he who believes in me." The Scripture says, "From within him there shall flow rivers of living water." St. John then adds: "He said this, however, of the Spirit whom they who believed in him were to receive; for the Spirit had not yet been given, since Jesus had not yet been glorified" (Jn 7:37-39). The glorification of Christ was his entrance into the glory of God the Father, thanks to the spiritualization of his body, after his Resurrection, as we have seen in the preceding chapter.

Once our Lord entered into the glory of his Father, the time came for the outpouring of the Holy Spirit, as St. Peter told the people at Jerusalem, on the morning of Pentecost: "This Jesus God has raised up, and we are all witnesses of it. Therefore, exalted by the right hand of God, and receiving from the father the promise of the Holy Spirit, he has poured forth this Spirit which you see and hear. For David did not ascend into heaven, but he says himself, "The Lord said to my Lord: Sit thou at my right hand, until I mke thy enemies thy footstool" (Ac 2:32-35).

At first reading the above words may surprise us. How could St. Peter say that "exalted by the right hand of God" (i.e., once he arose from the dead and entered into the glory of his Father), Jesus received from the Father "the promise of the Holy Spirit?" Didn't he possess him from all eternity, as the uncreated Son of God? As the incarnated Son, didn't he receive the Spirit already in fullness from the first instant of his conception in the womb of Mary? Didn't he receive a new anointing of the Spirit on the day of his baptism? There is no doubt about that. However, what St. Peter means is that the humanity of Christ, his body especially, was fully and totally spiritualized only after his Resurrection and Ascension. It was only then that his body was completely animated by the Holy Spirit and glorified. Christ's glorious entry into the Holy Trinity permitted him to return to his disciples spiritually, and with him bring the Holy Spirit.

As long as he dwelt on earth, in his *natural* body, Christ was *with* his disciples, but not *in* them. His presence in their midst was exterior to them, because his natural (physical) body subjected him to physico-chemical laws, which prevented him from entering *into* them. He would be able to do that only if his body were free from these laws, namely, a *spiritual* body. That is why he died and left the world. That is why, on the eve of his death, he said to his disciples: "It is expedient for you that I depart" (Jn 16:7). Like St. Peter's words, these words of our Lord surprise at first reading and seem difficult to understand. They, in fact, surprised the disciples unpleasantly, and made them sad. When they heard about his going away, they kept silent, and as St. John writes, "sorrow filled their hearts" (16:6). Our Lord had once said, in answer to the disciples of John the Baptist, who were scandalized that his own followers did not fast: "Can the wedding guests mourn as long as the bridegroom is with them? But the days will come when the bridegroom shall be taken away from them, and then they will fast" (Mt 9:15).

Jesus wanted his Apostles to be happy at the moment of the final parting. "If you loved me,'" He told them, "you would indeed rejoice that I am going to the Father" (Jn 14:28). Jesus, however, pointed out to them another reason for joy. It was profitable for them too, because freed from his natural (material) body, he would be able to be "in them," according to his words: "Yet a little while and the world no longer sees me (material absence). But you see me, for I live and you shall live. In that day (the day of Pentecost) you will know that I am in my Father, and you in me, and I in you (spiritual presence)" (Jn 14:19-20).

On the morning of the Jewish festival of Pentecost, fifty days after the Resurrection of Our Lord, there took place the outpouring of the Holy Spirit, of the Love with which Jesus is loved by the Father and which he returns unceasingly to his Father. The disciples were filled with this Spirit to the point of becoming inebriated.

Free of the restrictions of his natural (physical) body, then, Christ becomes present spiritually in the person who receives him by faith and love: and the Lord communicates to him the Holy Spirit: Love in Person. As Christ was sent by the Father, so the Spirit is sent by the Father and the Son, according to these words of Jesus: "The Holy Spirit whom the Father will send;" and "The Holy Spirit whom I will send from the Father" (Jn 14:26; 15:26). St. Paul wrote "The Holy Spirit whom God has abundantly poured out upon us through Jesus Christ, our Savior" (Tt 3:6). In becoming present spiritually in the Christian, Christ also communicates to him the Father, as well as the Spirit. Thus he said to his disciples: "If anyone love me, he will keep my word, and my Father will love him, and we will come to him, and make our abode with him" (Jn 14:23).

Now we are able to understand better the words of our Lord: "If I do not go, the Advocate will not come to you, but if I go, I will send him to you" (Jn 16:7). And also the words of St. Peter: "Exalted by the right hand of God, and receiving from the Father the promise of the Holy Spirit, he has poured forth the Spirit which you see and hear" (Ac 2:32-35).

This gift of the Spirit, which Christ made to his disciples on the day of Pentecost, could have been given on the very day of his Resurrection. In fact, Christ's Ascension, or his entrance into the Bosom of God, by which his glorification was fully realized, and with it the condition required for the sending of the Spirit, took place not forty days after his Resurrection but, as we learn from St. John, it happened on the morning of Easter itself. We read that the risen Jesus said to Mary Madgalene: "Go to my brethren and say to them, "I ascend to my Father and to your Father, to my God and your God" (Jn 20:17). We gather then that, before the visible Ascension, related by St. Luke in Acts, an event which closed the sensible manifestations of our Lord until his return at the end of time, there took place an *invisible* Ascension, revealed implicitly by St. John.

Immediately before his words to the Magdalene, cited above, by which she received the mission to announce this invisible Ascension to the Apostles, he said to her: "Do not touch me, for I have not yet ascended to my Father." "Do not touch me," is not a correct translation of the Latin, *"Noli me tangere."* Our Lord wanted to tell the affectionate Madgalene not to detain him and delay his entry into glory. St. John's account thus implies that the Lord ascended to his Father soon after he had spoken to Mary Madgelene. He could have sent the Holy Spirit on Easter. He didn't do so. Why?

One could give two reasons to explain why a period of fifty days elapsed before the event of Pentecost took place. First, it was necessary that the disciples have the time to realize fully the prodigious event of the Resurrection and to rejoice in it. Then, it was necessary that they prepare themselves for the outpouring of the Holy Spirit. For this was to be another event, distinct from the first and no less prodigious, and they needed time to grasp its importance and meaning. A preparation for the proper reception of this new event was necessary.

When Jesus had announced to his disciples the near coming of the Holy Spirit, he had told them not to go away from Jerusalem, but to wait there for the accomplishment of the promise of the Father. He was asking them to prepare themselves for the event. The sequel of the story permits us to guess in what this preparation consisted. By telling them not to leave Jerusalem, he asked of them not to return to their ordinary occupations, and to focus all their attention on the event announced to them. After quitting Mount of Olives after the Ascension of their Lord, the disciples returned to Jerusalem and retired to the Upper Room the *Cenacle,* where they were staying. "On the day of Pentecost, they were all together in the same place" (Ac 2:1). We can infer from this that the preparation of the disciples to the coming of the Holy Spirit consisted in unanimity of hearts and recollection in prayer. "All these with one mind continued steadfastly in prayer with the women and with Mary, the mother of Jesus, and with his brethren" (Ac 1:14).

The communion in love was asked for by the essentially communal character of pentecostal grace. The Holy Spirit was to descend not only on each of the disciples individually but also collectively on an assembly of which he was to make a spiritual unity. On the day of Pentecost the Church, whose foundation had already been laid, was definitevely built. Present were women, of whom one was Mary, and of many disciples, in addition to the Apostles. This shows that the Church will be composed by the hierarchy and the laity: men and women. The presence of Mary, expressly mentioned, underscores the important role that she will play in the Church, and first of all in the realization of the promise of the Father. In her prayer of incomparable efficacity, the prayer of all rose to the Father, and in her person, the whole community offered itself to receive the Holy Spirit.

This community assembled in the Cenacle around Mary, waiting for the irruption of the Spirit, had for its main occupation prayer: "they continued steadfastly in prayer." Without doubt, they prayed the Psalms, hymns and canticles, hence, the prayer of praise and thanksgiving, but also the prayer of petition, asking for the Holy Spirit, perhaps recalling what the Lord had once said: "If you, evil as you are, know how to give good gifts to your children, how much more will your heavenly Father give the Good Spirit to those who ask for it" (Lk 11:13).

This steadfastness in prayer must have had for its effect to make the hearts of the disciples more receptive and open for the gift of the Holy spirit. In fact, on the one hand, the prayer of petition expresses the free acceptance of what God desires to give but to respect our freedom he does not give unless one asks of him. This prayer, when animated by trust, puts the soul in a state of greater receptivity to the gifts of God. The man who asks recognizes his indigence and the need he has for the grace of God, and at the same time he declares his faith in the riches, goodness and almighty power of him to whom he addresses the petition.

The persevering prayer of the disciples had another effect: it helped them to enter more deeply into themselves and thus to permit the grace of Pentecost to transform them interiorly, and to let the Holy Spirit enter in them more intimately.

To this double preparation of the disciples to the descent of the Spirit, we should add the intercession of the Son. During the ten days which intervened between Ascension and Pentecost a mystery was accomplished, of which Scripture lets us see a glimpse. In Hebrews we read that our Lord "entered into the Holies;" "that he appears now before the face of God," "to intercede in favor of his brethren" (9:12, 24; 7:25). The glorified Lord, clothed with the fullness of his Priesthood, begins his role of intercessor by asking the Father to send the Holy Spirit. He thus fulfills the promise he had made to his Apostles on the eve of his death: "I will ask the Father, and he will give you another Advocate to dwell with you forever, the Spirit of truth" (Jn 14:16).

Realization of the Promise, Pentecost

When God the Father judged that the preparation of the disciples for the outpouring of his Spirit had ended, he granted the prayer of his Son and he fulfilled his promise. And Pentecost happened:

> *And when the days of Pentecost were drawing to a close, they (the disciples) were all together in one place. And suddenly there came a sound from heaven, as of a violent wind blowing, and it filled the whole house where they were sitting. And there appeared to them parted tongues as of fire, which settled upon each of them. And they were all filled with the Holy Spirit and began to speak in foreign tongues, even as the Holy Spirit prompted them to speak (Ac 2:1-4).*

The Holy Spirit irrupted in the Cenacle in a sudden, violent and full manner. "Suddenly," says St. Luke. The suddenness of the coming of the Holy Spirit underscores the sovereign liberty with which he operates. "The wind blows where it will, and thou hearest its sound but dost not know where it comes or where it goes. So is everyone who is born of the Spirit," our Lord said to Nicodemus.

"The violent wind blowing" manifests the presence of the Holy Spirit whom Holy Scripture and especially our Lord have described under the symbol of the wind, whose violence that day signifies one of his characteristics: his power. The Holy Spirit came to bring about the interior, radical transformation of the whole human being. He effected this transformation by recasting man in the fire of his love. Jesus had said: "John indeed baptized with water, but you shall be baptized with the Holy Spirit" (Ac 1:3). In other words, since to baptize means to plunge into, you will be transformed by a plunge into the Spirit, precisely *into the fire of his love*. This transformation, this total recasting, demanded the special intervention of him who is the power of God personified: the Holy Spirit. "I indeed baptize you with water," John the Baptist declared. "But one mightier than I is coming. He will baptize you with the Holy Spirit and with fire" (Lk 3:16).

The sound of this violent wind blowing, says St. Luke, filled the whole house. This particular is another characteristic of the Holy Spirit: the plenitude with which he gives himself.

"The tongues of fire" symbolize the fiery words, full of assurance and persuasion, with which the Apostles will thenceforth announce Jesus Christ and his message. They also symbolize, and above all, the ardent love and zeal with which they will burn for the service of God and man, and which their words of fire will be the expression.

If the disciples were going to burn with this love and zeal, and which will express this love and zeal in fiery words, it was because of the overflowing life of the Spirit of love, of which they will henceforth live. St. Luke writes, in fact, that "they were filled with the Holy Spirit." And their Lord had told them: "You will be filled with the Holy Spirit." The fullness of the gift, as I have pointed out above, is a characteristic of the outpouring of the Spirit. God does not give himself in a measure. "God," will say St. Paul, "has abundantly poured out upon us the Holy Spirit through Jesus Christ, our Savior" (Tt 3:6).

This fullness is also a fullness of action, which spreads outside. The first effect of this was manifested by the gift of tongues. St. Luke writes that the disciples "began to speak in foreign tongues," and that the people of various nationalities that happened to be in Jerusalem who heard the disciples speak, said: "We have heard them speaking in our own language of the wonderful works of God."

The gift of tongues, or a striking display of religious enthusiasm, was one of the ways in which the outpouring of the Spirit spread on to the crowd. The Holy Spirit was given in view of the proclamation of the good news of salvation, brought to the world by Christ, and in view of the witness to be given for him, where our Lord told his disciples that they would give him this testimony: "You shall be witness for me in Jerusalem and in all Judea and Samaria and even to the very ends of the earth" (Ac 1:8; cf Jn 15:26-27; Mt 10:18-20). Various charisms are mentioned in the New Testament; these were given by the Holy Spirit to strenghten the witness for Christ. In Hebrews, for example, we read: "The salvation was first announced by the Lord and was confirmed unto us by those who heard him; God also, according to his own will, bore witness by signs and wonders, and by manifold powers, and by impartings of the Holy Spirit" (2:4).

Our Lord himself, before his Ascension, had told his disciples about the various charisms they were about to be given, among which he mentioned "speaking in tongues:"

Go into the whole world and preach the gospel to every creature. He who believes and is baptized shall be saved, but he who does not believe shall be condemned. And these signs shall attend those who believe: in my name they shall cast out devils; they shall speak in new tongues; they shall take up serpents; and if they drink any deadly thing, it shall not hurt them; they shall lay hands upon the sick and they shall get well (Mk 16:15-18).

Later in this chapter, we will hear St. Peter affirm the realization of the prophecy of Joel about these signs and wonders, on the day of Pentecost.

The gift of tongues, or "speaking, praying and singing in tongues," is then one of the many charisms given by the Holy Spirit to confirm the announcement of the good tidings of salvation of Jesus Christ. What is the gift of tongues? To answer this question, it is necessary first to speak of charisms in general, of which tongues is one. The Gospels, Acts, St. Peter, St. Paul affirm repeatedly the existence in the Church of an action of the Holy Spirit of a special order, to which the name of charism has been given.

I have just cited a passage of St. Mark about these charisms. St. Matthew, on his part, says that these charisms were granted by Jesus to his disciples even before the solemn coming of the Holy Spirit: "Having summoned his twelve disciples," says St. Matthew, "Jesus gave them the power over unclean spirits, to cast them out, and to cure every kind of disease and infirmity" (Mt 10:1; cf. 10:7-8). St. Luke shows the disciples exercising these charisms: "The seventy-two disciples," he writes, "returned with joy, saying, "I was watching Satan fall as lightning from heaven. Behold, I have given you power to tread upon serpents and scorpions, and over all the might of the enemy; and nothing shall hurt you" (Lk 10:17-19).

The Acts of the Apostles certifies in numerous places the existence of charisms among the Apostles and the first Christians. In the story of Pentecost, one of these charisms, speaking in tongues, was involved. Later in Acts, it is stated twice that, "Many wonders and signs were done by means of the Apostles in Jerusalem" (2:43; 5:12). Of St. Stephen, it is said that "full of grace and power, he was working great wonders and signs among his people" (Ac 6:8). And in his first Letter, St. Peter says the following about charisms: "According to the gift that each has received, administer it to one another as good stewards of the manifold grace of God" (1 P 4:10-11). However, it is St. Paul who speaks about them the most:

Just as on one body we have many members, yet all members have not the same function, so we, the many, are one body in Christ, but severally members one of another. But we have gifts differing according to the grace that has been given us, such as prophecy to be according to the proportion of faith; or ministry, in ministering; or he who teaches, in teaching; he who exhorts, in exhorting; he who gives, in simplicity; he who presides, with carefulness; he who shows mercy, with cheerfulness (Rm 12:4-8).

Walk in a manner worthy of the calling with which you were called, with all humility and meekness, with patience, bearing with one another in love, careful to preserve the unity of the Spirit in the bond of peace: one body and one Spirit, even as you were called in one hope of your calling...

> *But to each of us grace was given according to the measure of Christ's bestowal. . . He himself gave some men as apostles, and some as prophets, others again as evangelists, and others as pastors and teachers, in order to perfect the saints for a work of ministry, for building up the body of Christ (Ep 4:1-13).*

> *Now there are varieties of gifts, but the same Spirit; and there are varieties of ministries, but the same Lord; and there are varieties of workings, but the same God, who works all things in all. Now the manifestations of the Spirit is given to everyone for profit. To one through the Spirit is given the utterance of wisdom; and to another the utterance of knowledge, according to the same Spirit; to another faith, in the same Spirit; to another the gift of healing, in the one Spirit; to another the working of miracles; to another prophecy; to another the distinguishing of spirits; to another various kinds of tongues; to another interpretation of tongues. But all these things are the work of one and the same Spirit, who allots to everyone according as he will (1 Cor 12:4-11).*

It follows from all these texts that, in additon to the graces which "justify" man, namely, which sanctify, divinize and make him pleasing to God, such as habitual or divinizing grace: faith, hope and charity, the seven gifts of the Holy Spirit, there exist graces attributed in a special way to the same Spirit, as the first, but which are given for the good of the Christian community, and not directly for the sanctification of the beneficiary. These are the "spiritual gifts," or "charisms."

The word charism comes from the Greek term *kharisma*, related to *kharis* which means "grace." Charisms are called *"gratiae gratis datae"*: graces given gratuitously, to distinguish them from *"gratia gratum faciens,"* the grace making the receiver pleasing, or sanctifying and divinizing grace, which is directly ordained to the sanctification of the person who receives it. This term of *"gratis datae"* does not mean that the grace *"gratum faciens"* is not gratuitous like the charisms. It is just as much the term has for its only reason to underscore that, contrary to sanctifying grace which is given directly for the sanctification of the beneficiary, charisms are given for the benefit of the community, for the "edification" of the Church, in the double sense of the word: for her construction and for the growth of fraternal love. The beneficiary of the gift serves mainly as an instrument for the total good of community.

In fact, in itself the presence of a charism in an individual is not necessarily a sign of the presence in him of sanctifying grace, a proof of his union with God, even less of his holiness. St. Paul says: "If I should speak with the tongues of men and of angels, but do not have love, I have become as sounding brass or a tinkling cymbal" (1 Cor 13:1). And Jesus uttered these stern words: "Not everyone who says to me, 'Lord, Lord,'shall enter the kingdom of heaven; but he who does the will of my Father in heaven. . . Many will say to me in that day, 'Lord, Lord, did we not prophesy in thy name, cast out devils in thy name, and work many miracles in thy name?' And then I will declare to them, 'I never knew you. Depart from me, you workers of iniquity' " (Mt 7:21-23). That is why, he said to his disciples: "Do not rejoice in this, that the spirits are subject to you; rejoice rather in this, that your names are written in heaven" (Lk 10:20). This is why, after he had enumerated to the Corinthians the various charisms, St. Paul adds: "I point out to you a yet more excellent way" (1 Cor. 12:31); and then he shows them the way of love, which presupposes the possession of sanctifying grace (cf. Cor. 13:1-13).

What I have just said about charisms, of course does not mean that these graces never sanctify in any way those who are favored with them. These charisms have for their end the edification of the Mystical Body, the Church, and also to make love grow in her. This goal can only be reached by the flourishing and growth of divinizing grace in the members of the Body of Christ. It is to be expected that being ordained for the sanctification of the community, charisms will begin by sanctifying those who are favored with them In fact, according to St. Paul, there are charisms ordained for the personal edification of the receiver: "He who speaks in a tongue edifies himself," he says, "but he who prophesies edifies the Church" (1 Cor 14:4).

Charisms are directly ordained for the benefit of the community rather than for the good of the beneficiary. If sometimes they show in the latter the presence of sanctifying grace, and even his holiness, their principal role is to manifest the intervention of the Holy Spirit, and to serve for the propagation of the Christian faith among the "infidels," as well as for the spiritual growth of the faithful. The charisms give then testimony for Christ and to his Gospel by manifesting the dynamic action of the Spirit. Indeed, "a Church which would not recognize the place and the action of charisms in her daily life," writes Cardinal Suenens, "would be an atrophied Church, severed from her profound animation."

Besides the extraordinary gifts, there are ordinary charisms, with which Christians are favored whether by the character imprinted in them in Baptism and Confirmation, or by virtue of their state in life: celibate life, conjugal life, consecrated life; whether by virtue of the ministries that they have to exercise in the Church, or by virtue of their vocation in the field of evangelization, of catechesis, and of Catholic Action in all its forms. Every personal talent can be used as a charism to spread love and understanding in the world. Every Christian may be favored by one or more charisms which, under the dynamic action of the Spirit, can be used for the good of his brother, with enthusiastic joy.

The Holy Spirit often uses the natural talents of the faithful and the charisms, in the restricted meaning of the word, have always existed in the Church, though they became rare for several centuries. Since a dozen or more years ago, charisms have begun to flourish again, as they did in the primitive Church, with the appearance of a movement called "the charismatic renewal."

To return to the event of Pentecost. Confronted by the extraordinary, and rather strange, phenomenon, the crowd gathered outside of the Cenacle reacted differently to it. Some were "amazed and marvelled;" others to explain away the unusual happening, said in mockery, "They are full of new wine." St. Peter refutes this explanation with a simple remark, saying: "These men are not drunk, as you suppose, for it is only the third hour of the day," i.e., nine o'clock in the morning, at that time not an hour for men to get drunk! Yet, the remarks of the mocking skeptics contained some truth, for exteriorly the disciples did give the impression of being intoxicated. Indeed, the outpouring of the Holy Spirit produced in them a veritable inebriation, but one of a different type, of which St. Peter showed the cause by citing the prophecy of Joel:

What is happening was announced by the prophet Joel:

'And it shall come to pass in the last days, says, the Lord, that I will pour forth my Spirit upon all flesh;
And your sons and your daughters shall prophesy, and your young men shall see visions, and your old men shall dream dreams.
And moreover upon my servants and upon my handmaids in those days will I pour forth my Spirit, and they shall prophesy
And I will show wonders in the heavens above and signs on the earth beneath. . . (Ac 2:16-21; cf Jl 3:1-5).

The "intoxication" with which the disciples were accused is not an exaltation of short duration. It is a continual enthusiasm fed by the permanent presence of the Spirit, and it transforms them. Till then, they were timid, even lax. Now they become fearless, capable of surmounting all obstacles and to face all persecutions, death itself, with an unfailing joy, fruit of the Spirit. "The disciples," writes St. Luke, speaking of Paul and Barnabas, who had just been expelled from a city, "continued to be filled with joy and with the Holy Spirit" (Ac 13:52). Before this, the same evangelist has narrated the episode of the arrest of the Apostles by the Sadducees, and their appearance before the members of the Sanhedrin: "Calling in the apostles and having them scourged, they charged them not to speak in the name of Jesus, and then let them go. So they departed from the presence of the Sanhedrin, rejoicing that they had been worthy to suffer disgrace for the name of Jesus" (Ac 5:40-41).

The "inebriation" of the Holy Spirit, is a "sober intoxication," which, instead of making one lose his head as does the intoxication produced by wine communicates a greater possession of oneself, a coolness and an extraordinary assurance as well as an overflowing joy. That's why St. Paul will say to the Christians of Ephesus: "Do not be drunk with wine, for in that is debauchery; but be filled with the

Spirit, speaking one to another in psalms and hymns and spiritual songs, singing and making melody in your hearts to the Lord, giving thanks always for all things in the name of our Lord Jesus Christ to God the Father" (Ep 5:18-20).

The joy, the enthusiasm and the soberness of this spiritual intoxication brought forth fruits immediately. In fact, following St. Peter's discourse to the crowd, many had "their hearts pierced," as St. Luke notes (Ac 2:37). They accepted his message and let themselves be baptized. "That day were added to the Church three thousand souls," thus St. Luke ends his account of Pentecost (Ac 2:37).

Having thus fulfilled the promise that he had made to give his Spirit in "the last times," God the Father will continue thenceforth, up to the end of time, to send him together with his Son, to men who will ask for the gift, to make them communicate in the divine life and love.

CHAPTER SIX

The Holy Spirit in the Work of Our Divinization

On the morning of the Jewish festival of Pentecost, the Holy Spirit was given by the Father and the Son to the newly-born Church, to be received not only collectively but also individually, by each person who was going to become member of this Church, through their faith in Christ. "If anyone thirst," had declared Jesus, "let him come to me and drink. He who believes in me, as the Scripture says: 'From within him there shall flow rivers of living water.' " St. John, who recorded these words, then adds: "He said this, however, of the Spirit whom they who believed in him were to receive" (Jn 7:37-39). It was to each of his disciples that he was addressing himself when he first told them about the Holy Spirit: "You shall know him, because he will dwell with you, and be in you" (Jn 14:17).

"He will be in you." The Holy Spirit was then sent in order to dwell in each of us who believes in Christ. He is in our whole being, in our soul and our body, dwelling there as in a temple. He is the guest of our soul. "Do you not know," asks St. Paul, "that you are the temple of God and that the Spirit of God dwells in you?" In another place, he says: "You are not carnal but spiritual, since the Spirit of God dwells in you" (Rm 8:9). Like our soul, our body too, is the temple of God, of the Holy Spirit in a special way. Again it is St. Paul who tells us so: "Do you not know that your body is the temple of the Holy Spirit, who is in you, whom you have from God" (1 Cor 6:19-20).

Dwelling in us, the Holy Spirit is unceasingly at work. First he transforms our being and divinizes it, making us partakers of the divine nature. Secondly he makes us to share the life of the Father and the Son, thanks to the union he establishes between Christ and us. Here we will consider the Holy Spirit's role in our divinization. In the next chapter, I shall speak of his role in our union with Jesus Christ.

The Essence of the Divine Plan: Our Divinization

The doctine of the divinization of men is the keystone of Christianity. It is also a truth that we forget too often, not to say, that we ignore completely. In fact, we have a tendency to reduce salvation to the mystery of the Redemption. We say that our Lord came in the world to redeem us, to expiate and delete our sins. This is true, but we omit to add the fact that he came above all to make us children of God, beings who participate in the nature of their Father: divinized beings.

Redemption is one thing, divinization another. Thus, if men had not sinned, they would have been called to partake in the divine nature, and would have achieved this goal, *in Christ,* without first having to be cured of the evils inflicted upon themselves by their rebellion and sins. It would not have been necessary for the Lord to die on the Cross to redeem them. But men did sin; hence, they needed to be purified of their sins, and to be rescued from the evils, resulting from their sins. This is the work of Redemption effected by Christ, the Savior. Therefore, we "give thanks with joy to God, the Father, who has made us worthy to share the lot of the saints in light. He has rescued us from the power of darkness and transferred us into the kingdom of his beloved Son, in whom we have redemption, the remission of our sins" (Col 1:12-14).

Here are some texts from the New Testament about the astonishing doctrine of our divinization, the real *good news,* the mystery or plan, "which," says St. Paul, "God foreordained before the world unto our glory. . . Eye has not seen nor ear heard, nor has it entered into the heart of man, what things God has prepared for those who love him" (1 Cor 1:7-9).

"Through our Savior Jesus Christ, God has granted us very great and precious promises, so that through them we may become *partakers of the divine"* (2 P 1:4). "Behold what manner of love the Father has bestowed upon us, that we should be called children of God, and such we are" (1 Jn 3:1).

St. Paul writes: "You know the graciousness of our Lord Jesus Christ—how being *rich,* he became *poor* for your sake, that by *his proverty you might become rich"* (2 Cor 8:9). In her Liturgy, the Church calls this exchange: *admirabile commercium:* "O wondrous exchange, the Creator of the human race, taking upon himself a body and a soul, has deigned to be born of a Virgin, and appearing here below as man has made us partakers of his divinity" (*First Vespers* of the Octave of Christmas). And in the Preface for Easter, she sings about the Word Incarnate "Who by his death destroyed our death and by his Resurrection restores us to life. And "Who ascended into heaven that he may make us partakers of his divinity" (*Preface* of the Ascension).

The Fathers never tired to talk about this gracious design of God: the divine exchange: "God in the beginning of time plants the vine of the human race," St. Irenaeus writes. "He loved this human race and purposed to pour his Spirit upon it to give it the adoption of sons" (Ad. Haer). "The Lord redeemed us by his blood," he says elsewhere; "he gave his soul for our souls and his flesh for our flesh, and sent forth the Spirit of the Father to bring about unity and communion between God and man. Through the Spirit *he gave God to men,* and through his Incarnation he *raised man to God"* (Ad. Haer.).

St. Hilary writes: "God, the only-begotten One, is born of the Virgin, so that he may raise man, in himself to the dignity of God. This mystery is not for God, but for us. God gains nothing by our 'assumption' (by taking us into himself), but his voluntary *abasement* is our *exaltation.* God loses none of his divinity, while man is enabled to become God" *(De Trinitate).*

St. Athanasius: "Such is God's love for men that he willed to become a Father, by grace, of those whom he created. Now since they are creatures, they could not become sons unless they received the Spirit of him who is the natural and true Son of God. Therefore was the Word made flesh, to render man capable of receiving the divinity" *(Contra Arianos).*

St. Cyril of Alexandria: "Remember well this profound and great mystery. You hear how the Word, the only-begotten Son of God, has been made like us, in order that we too may become like to him, as far as this is possible for our nature and as far as the plan of our supernatural renewal will permit. He lowered himself in order to raise to his own dignity, that which is base by nature; though by nature he is God and Son, *he took the form of a slave that he might transform those who are slaves by nature into the glory of adoption* according to his likeness. He became man, that we in turn may be made Gods and sons" (In Joh).

And St. Leo the Great: "Learn, O Christian, how great is our dignity! And having been made a *partaker of the divine nature,* return not, by a reversion unworthy of your race, to your former baseness. Remember who is your Head and of what Body you are a member! Remember that having been snatched from the power of darkness, you have been transported into the light of the Kingdom of God. By the Sacrament of Baptism you have become a temple of the Holy Spirit; drive not away from you, by a depraved conduct, so great a Guest" (I Sermon *In Nativitate Domini*).

I should like to end my quotations with two of Maurice Blondel on this beautiful doctrine, which he calls "the supreme enigma to philosophy, and the inexhaustible treasure to the believer, the good news *par excellence,* the news which is ever new":

> *When, to summarize the glad tidings, St. John writes,* credimus caritati, *we believe in love, he meant by these words that the incomparable privilege of Christianity, is the revelation and the realization of this superior order, which he calls divine philanthropy: God so loved the world that he has given his only-begotten Son, that the eternal Word having become flesh, man might be really adopted and divinized by this Mediator.*

Elsewhere he wrote:

> *Now here we touch an essential mystery of divine revelation: what appeared incredible, what seemed impossible, what men, too many to them, have called "folly and scandal," is that Revelation presents us as the goal of the divine plan of creation, the common work of the Three divine Persons, the decision to make man according to God's likeness, and by the mediation of the eternal Word, made Man, to raise (and restore) man, so poor in his flesh, and guilty in his rebellious pride, the divine level, giving him the grace of divine union:* consortium naturae divinae.

We know from Scripture that "God created man in his image and likeness," namely, that he invited man by a totally gratuitous liberality to participate in his very nature. God was not content to create man only as man; in other words, to give him the natural life, which his nature requires in its physical and metaphysical definition of a nature composed essentially of a body and of a soul endowed with intellect and free will, capable to know and to love. God did more. From the very beginning and out of pure love, he raised man to a state, much superior than his nature as man, without man having any right to this (supernatural) elevation.

To profit by this elevation, which is no other than a participation in the divine nature, man had to make a choice. This supernatural destiny involves a condition which could not be avoided. The participation of the divine nature is a *grace,* a gift that God offers to man, out of pure love. Now love does not impose itself, it only offers. It is a gift. And precisely because it is a gift, it wants the free consent of the loved one. God, consequently, could not make man a god without his acceptance.

The Fathers talk about the powerlessness and the humility of God, that God imposed upon himself in creating man free, hence, capable of checkmaking God's almighty power, of frustrating the divine plan. From this the Fathers have not hesitated to call God's love for man a veritable "folly." Faced with the offer of the gift of divinization, made by God to him, man had to consent to it, and to cooperate with the grace of God to make himself worthy to benefit from this totally astonishing gift, of being "partakers of the divine nature."

We learn from the Bible that the first man and woman refused this gift. They refused by disobeying God's commandment not to eat of the fruit of the tree of the knowledge of good and evil. From the biblical narrative, we learn that they disobeyed God precisely in order to make themselves gods, to be like God. Satan said to them: "God knows that when you eat of the fruit of the tree, your eyes will be opened and you will be like God, knowing good and evil" (Gn 3:5). To be like God. Weren't Adam and Eve already that? Yes, they were. However, there exist two types of likeness: a likeness of absolute equality, and a likenes by participation.

It is clear that in creating man and woman in his likeness, God did not intend to make them similar to him by a likeness that would make them his exact equals. He would have had to give them his nature, such as it is in itself, with its own proper mode of existence, in virtue of which God exists by himself, with a total and absolute independence. What scholastic philosophers call by the word *aseitas: a se,* by itself. God's nature is *to be: to exist.* No cause, no justification is needed for God to be.

We can easily see from this that God does not give his nature to anybody. "I am the Lord, this is my name; my glory I give to no other, nor my praise to idols" (Is 42:8). Understand "my divinity" by the words, "my glory." Moreover, he could not do it, for he would cease to be what he is, God, since then there would be two or more gods, and consequently, there would not be any at all. In fact, unity, in the sense of unicity (oneness), is an essential attribute of God, since the existence of two metaphysical absolutes is inconceivable because one could pose himself only by opposing himself to the other and thus limiting him by this very opposition. God is the Unique, the ONE. "I, I alone, am God, and there is no god besides me" (Dt 32:39; cf. Is 45:35).

But it is possible for God to give to man, through pure love, a certain participation in his nature. That is what he did when he created man. Consequently it is not for having wanted this likeness by participation in the divine nature that man sinned (Original Sin), since this likeness had been given to him at the moment of his creation.

Can we say then that man sinned in seeking a likeness of absolute equality with God? This would seem impossible, at first sight. To desire such a likeness would seem to be sought by no person; no spirit is capable of similar folly, one would think. Nevertheless, it seems that we can assert that man sinned (originally) by wanting to be equal to God. He wanted what God didn't want to give to him, what God could not give, namely his nature of which the essential attribute is unicity (Oneness). In fact, man tried to be God: he wanted to be autonomous like God, to depend on himself alone. That is why he refused to offer to God the fruit of the tree of the knowledge of good and evil. This offering would have constituted for him an act of acknowledgement towards God—an acknowledgement not only in the sense of thanksgiving, but also and by the very fact, a recognition of dependence. This attitude made Cardinal Jean Danielou say: "He who will go to hell will be he who will refuse absolutely to give thanks; who will say: I prefer to be eternally wretched rather than to have to say thanks to God." It is why the first sin of man was inspired by pride, i.e., by love of his own excellence, because he wanted to be not only something more than what God had made him, but God himself.

What permits us to assert this is that it is pure folly to pretend to be similar to God with an absolute likeness, even to the point of wanting to do away with him by substituting man for God. Friedrick Nietzsche wrote: "God is dead," in *The gay science:*

> *Whither is God? he cried: I will tell you.* We have killed him—*you and I. All of us are his murderers. But how did we do this? How could we drink up the sea? . . . Do we smell nothing as yet of the divine decomposition? Gods too, decompose.* God is dead. *God remains dead and we killed him. How shall we comfort ourselves, the murderers of all murderers? What was the holiest and mightiest of all that the world has yet owned has bled to death under our knives: who will wipe this blood off us?. . . Is not the greatness of this deed too great for us?* Must we ourselves not become gods *simply to appear worthy of it? There has never been a greater deed; and whoever is born after us—for the sake of this deed he will belong to a higher history than all history hitherto.*

And Karl Marx:

> *No being is independent in its own eyes, unless it is sufficient unto itself; and it is not sufficient unto itself, unless it holds its own existence from itself. A man who lives by the grace of another, considers himself dependent. But I live completely by the grace of another when I owe to him, not only the conservation of my life, but also its very origin and source. The source of my life is of necessity outside myself if I am not my own creator. For this it is difficult to rid the popular imagination of the idea of creation. The socialist, on the other hand, since for him all history is no more than the*

creation of man by work, no more than the gradual overcoming of nature by man, possesses the visible and irrefutable proof of the fact that he is his own creator.

This goal (or rather illusion) is not only that of Marxist materialism, the most conscious and ruthless effort to set up on earth a society where every trace of belief in God and the supernatural has been abolished, for it is equally the avowed goal of every materialism. An American writer, speaking about the technological wonders of the modern world, says "the appetite of power that technology has aroused aims at establishing control over the whole of creation, considered up to now as immutable. The clouds, the wind, vegetables, the animal and the immense sidereal spaces must submit to man. The aim is to conquer the "throne of God" and *to substitute man for the divinity."*

Jean-Paul Sartre is seized by this folly. "What expresses best," he writes, "the fundamental project of human reality is that *man is the being whose project is to be God.* To be man means to reach toward being God. Or if one prefers, man is fundamentally the desire to be God. Man in his very emergence is being borne toward God as toward his limit." Also for Sartre God must die in order that man may live, for *"if God exists man is nothing."*

Finally, Francis Jeanson, in *La foi d'un incroyant,* says: "The universe is perhaps a machine to make gods . . . and the human species is capable to incarnate God and to realize him, to put an end to him by inventing our own humanity." For Jeanson, like Sartre, human reality consists, or posits itself, in the affirmation of himself, and the rejection of the *Wholly-Other* or God. Man's liberty, as well as his person, affirms itself in the rejection of every dependence. It is radical, total autonomy.

To want to do without God, not to depend on him, means to sever relations with him, and therefore to annihilate himself. Our existence as creatures has not in itself its own principle or origin. To exist for a creature means to be only for God, the Creator. The human person is wholly relative to God, and it affirms itself all the more by being dependent on him. The relation of man to God, his dependence to God is consequently the very constitutive element of his being.

Man cannot ever succeed in his desire to cease depending on God, since man having been created, he can exist *only* by being dependent on God whether man likes it or not.

Technical and scientific progress has given man the consciousness of his power, and he has become intoxicated with it. He really seems to think and feel that he is self-sufficient and can dispense with any help from God. But without God, man is nothing; without God man can only destroy himself. And it seems that he will destroy himself, even if he has to use those very technological devices he invented for building the earthly Paradise. Wanting to be self-sufficient, contemporary man faces total thermonuclear annihilation. Contemporary man as "a Steppenwolf," as a German writer put it, "hovers restlessly hither and thither in the loveless desert that is Western civilization and cries hideously his hunger and thirst for God he has killed?"

Though disordered and insane, this desire of auto-divinization is also a poignant phenomenon, a nostalgic obsession and unconscious yearning for this God that they think is *dead*. However, without falling in the exaggeration expressed by the thinkers quoted above, all of us, unceasingly tend to deify ourselves in one way or another; and that "the permanent temptation," as S. de Dietrich writes, "the true diabolical temptation of man is to make himself God. And let us not think right way of the megalomania of certain modern rulers and other mighty ones of the world, intoxicated with pride and with the thirst for power. To make oneself God, is to take oneself as center of one's universe, whether it be great or small, to seek one's own glory rather than the glory of God, to want to make one's own life instead of receiving it from the hands of God, in short wanting to belong to oneself instead of belonging to God."

The first man and woman sinned in seeking to be independent, to be like God. They had the arrogant pretension to make themselves equal to God. This is the likeness that they wanted, and God did not want to give them.

Nature of Our Divinization

What is then the likeness to which God has called man, and that man lost by his fault, and that Jesus Christ restored to him by the power of the Holy Spirit? In what does our divinization consist?

The original destiny to which man is called left in human nature a desire of deification, a desire that we meet in the ancient pagan philosophers and also, as we have seen in modern thinkers, though more or less disordered and rebellious. The ancient philosophers saw the perfection of man exactly in a certain deification or assimilation of man to God, by his intellect which by contemplation attains in some way divine thought, and divine joy. However, how distant and imperfect is their conception compared to the supernatural divinization gained for us by Christ! The assimilation to God was either superficial, or a total blending—thus lowering God, grounding him in his creation. As to the modern thinkers, we have seen, what their auto-deification means.

The true deification, the one which makes man truly "a partaker of the divine nature," and which takes into account both the existence and the transcendence of God, is only possible, in the state of fallen humanity, because God is a Triune God, and because of the Incarnation—mysteries which human reason is incapable of conceiving, and which can reject. It was necessary that there be in God a Son, consubstantial to the father, perfectly equal to him, and a God himself (not as Greek philosophers thought: a *Logos* or *Nous*) engendered indeed by the Unique God, yet an inferior or a "second god," a kind of superior creature and the principle of all creation. It was necessary, secondly, that this only-begotten Son become man and by his sacrificial death shatter the obstacle of sin—something the ancient thinkers were incapable of imagining. It was necessary, finally, that the Son be united through his human nature in order to make men partakers in his divinity.

It follows that divinization, according to Christianity, differs essentially from pantheistic divinization.

According to pantheism, the world is ontologically consubstantial to God, and souls are particles or modalities of the divine substance—they are therefore divine by nature from the beginning; they proceed or flow eternally and necessarily from the One or the Absolute. "Wisdom," writes M. Cl. Tresmontant, "lies in recognizing the substantial identity between the individual me and the absolute Me, between the individual soul and the universal Soul, between the atman and the Brahman. Salvation consists in bringing about the return of the apparent multiple to the One from which the many proceed and from which they have fallen to melt in the one in the unique divine substance, in losing the individuality which is the mark of the fall" (*Lettre*, Sept.-Oct. 1962).

According to Christianity, man is called to partake of the life of God, by *graçe*. He is invited to be a "partaker of the divine nature," as St. Peter writes. St. Paul says that in the end "God will be all in all" (1 Cor 15:28). We must beware of confusing with pantheism the words of St. Paul who affirms the immanence of God in the whole creation, his presence in all creatures, and also affirm God's transcendence. According to Christianity, divinization is brought about without confusion or blending of either the nature or of the persons. The personal distinction remains and makes possible love. On the other hand, the Apostle does not say that many came forth from the substance of God, or that he is ontologically consubstantial to God from the origins. Only the Word, and hence the Word incarnated, Jesus Christ, is God by nature and possesses orginally the same and one divine substance.

To him only, the Father communicates his nature which becomes, without division, diminution nor multiplication, the proper substance of Christ, and which makes our Lord to be consubstantial and equal to the Father. Our participation to the divine nature, which makes of us divinized beings, is not the consubstantiality of our soul with God, the ideal of all pantheistic mysticisms, but only a *certain* likeness, which makes of us, not equal to God, but deiform beings or *similar* to God. It is not an emanation or a flowing in us of the divine nature, nor of a certain reality (*divine energies)* which exists in God and which from God passes in us. It is the communication to our soul, not of a divine particle, but of the image of God, comparable to the communication of the imprint of a seal on the wax, as the Fathers of the Church say, following St. Paul.

Though we remain creatures, though we do not become God and we do not blend with him in the unity of being and person, we are really divinized by a substantial transformation which, without depriving us of our substance, unites us to God with a substantial union, not in the sense of a mingling of natures, but of a union of nature to nature. The Father divinizes our soul by making it like to himself through the spiritual contact of the nature of his Son, which is his own nature, with the nature of our soul, like the wax is made similar to the imprint of the seal through the contact of the seal with the imprint.

This radical, essential transformation of our being, which effects our divinization, takes place at baptism. It consists in a change which establishes bewtween the Trinitarian Persons and us *new* relations. These relations arise from a new knowledge and a new love that this Sacrament communicates to us. This new knowledge will permit us to know God and his creatures as God knows himself and his creatures: the theological virtue of *faith*. This new love enables us to love God and his creatures as God loves himself and them: the theological virtue of *charity*. To these two virtues is attached a third, *hope,* which is the desire of the faith to know God more and more, and the desire of charity to unite with God with a union ever more intimate.

Faith and charity transform interiorly our intelligence and heart and make us capable of knowing and loving like God. Only a difference exists, but it is a pure difference of degree, not of nature. Of degree, for as St. Paul says: "Now I know in part, then I shall know even as I have been known"; and "We see through a mirror in an obscure manner but then face to face" (1 Cor 13:2). St. John on his part writes: "Beloved, now we are children of God, and it has not yet appeared what we shall be. We know that, when he appears, we shall be like to him, for we shall see him just as he is" (1 Jn 3:2). Difference, I repeat, of degree not of nature, because faith and charity are not only an objective communication of the thought and the love of God, but also and above all, as we shall see, an interior communion and a real participation in this thought and this love.

A state of intimacy, a communion with the Father, the Son and the Holy Spirit, established by knowledge and love: such is our divinization. "In that day," Jesus said, "you will know that I am in my Father and you in me and I in you" (Jn 14:20). And to his Father, he said: "That all may be one, even as thou, Father, in me and I in thee, that they also may be one in us. . .And the glory that thou hast given me, I have given to them, that they may be one, even as we are one: I in them and thou in me; that they may be perfected in unity" (Jn 17:21-23).

This communion with God, or the presence in us of the Three

divine Persons is not a static thing. Like the presence of each Person in the other Two, it is a dynamic divine activity, for it makes us participate in the wondrous circulation of Love of each toward the other Two. In our soul, thus inhabited by the Trinity, there takes place the eternal generation of the Son by the Father and the eternal spiration of the Spirit of Love by the Father and the Son.

Moreover, the presence of God in us makes us capable of participating in the proper activity of the divine Persons: we find ourselves marvellously associated to this generation and to this spiration, and are introduced, in a certain mysterious way, in the current of the Trinitarian life. Not only the Father generates continously in us his Son, and the Father and the Son breathe unceasingly in us their common Spirit of Love, but also, assimilated to the Son and to the Holy Spirit, we are continually, through participation, but really, being generated by the Father as children and breathed by the Father and the Son as objects of love; at the same time that we breathe unceasingly with the Son in union with the Father, their common Spirit of Love.

The life of the three divine Persons being one of mutual knowledge and love, by divinization we are made capable of knowing and loving them, as they know and love each other: we participate in the same knowledge with which they know Each Other, and in the same love they have One for the Others. The Father and the Son know us through the same knowledge with which they know themselves, in the Holy Spirit; on our part, we know the Father and the Son with this same mutual knowledge, through the same Holy Spirit, as our Lord declared: "I am the good shepherd, and I know mine and mine know me, even as the Father knows me and I know my Father" (Jn 10:14).

The Father and the Son love us with the same love they have One for the Other, in the Holy Spirit: "As the Father has loved me, I also have loved you," said Jesus to his disciples (Jn 15:9). And we love the Father and the Son with the same love they have for us, through the same Spirit: "You have loved them as you have loved me," Jesus prayed to his Father (Jn 17:23). "I have made known thy name, and will make it known, in order that the love with which thou hast loved me may be in them and I in them" (Jn 17:26).

The participation in the divine nature makes us also, like God, incorruptible and immortal. Speaking of the human body, at present subjected to corruption and death, St. Paul said: "Flesh and blood can obtain no part in the kingdom of God, neither shall corruption have any part in incorruption:" "This corruptible body must put on incorruption and this mortal body must put on immortality" (1 Cor 15:50, 53). Our divinization extends also to our body, as St. Paul writes: "Our Lord Jesus Christ will refashion the body of our lowliness conforming to the body of his glory" (Ph 3:21).

The glorious body of Christ is a spiritual body, an incorruptible and immortal body. Such will be ours too, after our resurrection. "Sown in corruption," says St. Paul, "it will rise in incorruption; sown in dishonor it will rise in glory; sown in weakness it will rise in power; sown a natural body it will rise a spiritual body" (1 Cor 15:42-44). It is true that our body is divinized "in hope:" we wait "for the redemption of our body" (Rm 8:23-24). But though our body is still "dead by reason of sin" (Rm 8:10), it participates in the divinization of our soul, in the sense that it becomes the temple of God, that it does not belong to us any longer but it belongs to God, and that it has been made a member of Christ and that, consequently, is called to holiness and to the glorification of God. (1 Cor 3:16-17; 6:13-20).

The Role of The Holy Spirit In Our Divinization

It is by the Holy Spirit, thanks to the union that he established between the Word incarnate and us, and to the participation that he gives us, in him, in the Trinitarian life that divinization is brought about.

Taking a body in the womb of Mary, the Word of God united himself to all humanity, according to the Eastern Fathers' thinking, and he divinized it. These Fathers found the starting point of their doctrine in these words of Christ: "The kingdom of heaven is like leaven, which a woman took and buried in three measures of flour, until all of it was leavened" (Mt 13:33). By uniting himself to a human nature, the Word has inserted himself in humanity. He deposited there a divine ferment, which will leaven eventually the whole dough; a ferment which has already extended its benefits to the whole human race, actually or potentially. Only those who exclude themselves knowingly and voluntarily do not profit from it. "When the Son of God, says St. Irenaeus, "took flesh, he *recapitulated* in himself the long series of man (took all humanity in himself) giving us salvation, re-doing the work of God destroyed by sin, in order that we re-find in Jesus Christ what we lost in Adam, the image and likeness of God."

St. Athanasius thus conceived the Incarnation as being a "contact," between the divine nature and the human nature, taken "in block," in its entirety. To understand fully all the force of these expressions, we should recall that, for St. Athanasius and the other Greek Fathers, the "human nature" must be taken in its neo-Platonist conception, and regard it not only as a logical abstraction, but as a reality in itself, an *ideal* without doubt, but an *objective thing,* existing distinctly in divine Thought, and from where we individual humans receive our being by "participation."

The union of the Word with the humanity of Christ is a union of the Word with "human nature," and we, individual human beings, share this divino-human "blending." St Athanasius further says: "The flesh is a terrestrial thing no longer, it becomes Word, 'it has become *word-fied,*' by the Word of God, who for us became flesh." St. Gregory of Nyssa speaks of the "blending" thusly: God has 'blended' himself with our nature so that, thanks to its 'blending' with the divine, our nature is divinized." And St. Cyril of Alexandria wrote "Through the action and the grace of his Spirit, he Son gives a new life to our spirit, and makes us partakers of his divine nature. Thus Christ becomes the bond who unites us to God the Father; by reattaching us to him, as man, he reattached us to God, as God."

However, it is not sufficient that the divine leaven is deposed in the human dough. It has to extend its divine action to each element ofthe human paste. It is not sufficient that the Word took human flesh and thus inserted himself in whole humanity in general; that all flesh became "word-fied," and hence divinized. It is also necessary that the divine nature, which has assumed the human nature of Christ and through it the whole of humanity, extends itself to each individual nature. In other words, each human being in particular, through a *personal* step or decision, unite himself effectively to the Word Incarnate.

Though every man is really divinized, he is insofar as he is man, part of human nature, and not insofar as he is such and such man. As an individual person, he is only divinized *virtually*. The divinization must *yet* win each individual man, just as the leaven leavens each particle of the dough, or as the sap gives life to each branch. This is done by the redemptive Passion of Christ, which shatters the obstacle of sin, the barrier to divinization. Each human being receives the divine sap or ferment through *faith* and the *Sacraments,* especially by Baptism and the Eucharist. These Sacraments apply to each person the benefits of the Redemption, and unite him actually to the Word, and hence divinize him.

It is the Father who deifies us; it is he who "chose us in Jesus Christ before the foundation of the world that we should be holy and without blemish in his sight in love" (Ep 1:4) and who renews us "according to the image of the Creator" (Col 3:9-10). However, it is in being formed according to the image of him, who is the Father's image, the Son who became man, died and rose again, that we are deified. And this renewal or divinization is the work of the Holy Spirit. In short, divinization is the work of the three Persons (of the *Triune* God) together, but attributed in a special way to the Holy Spirit. St. Gregory of Nyssa writes:

> *It is not at all because of the fact that he needs cooperation, that God has made all things through the Son. The Son too, it is not because of the fact that his power is to realize his designs, that he operates through the Holy Spirit. Not at all. However, the source of the power is the Father; the power of the Father is his Son; and the spirit of the power (of the Son) is the Holy Spirit. We must say, then, that in the production of all created things, everything which is a movement of the will: purpose, plan and communication of power, has its point of departure in the Father, is continued in the Son and is accomplished in the Holy Spirit. (De Spiritu Sancto)*

St. Cyril of Alexandria, on his part, writes: "It is the whole consubstantial Trinity, which operates in us our redemption or divinization. It is through the entire divine nature that involves itself in all its works. From this comes the reason why we give thanks and praise to only one Person, 'in bloc,' as it were. When we call God our Savior, it is not to the Father only, nor to the Son, nor to the Holy

Spirit only, that we praise and give thanks. It is really to the unique God that we attribute our salvation" (*In Joan*). And elsewhere he says: "If it is true that the Father has made all things by the Son, in the Holy Spirit . . . it would be absurd to distribute among the divine Persons the activities . . . of the unique and simple Godhead, instead of confessing that all things have been made by the Father through the Son in the Holy Spirit. The Son, in fact, being the Wisdom of the Father, the Father will do absolutely all things by the Son, as his Counselor, Wisdom and Power. It is evident, then, that since all things come from the unique God, they come from the Father, through the Son, in the Holy Spirit; (Adv. Nest.).

The purifying (redemptive) action, which is necessary to bring about our divinization, is accomplished by the Holy Spirit. "You have been washed," says St. Paul, "you have been sanctified, you have been justified in the name of our Lord Jesus Christ, and the Spirit of our God" (1 Cor 6:11). And we read in Titus: "When the goodness and kindness of God our Savior appeared, then not by reason of good works that we did ourselves, but according to his mercy, he saved us through the bath of regeneration and renewal by the Holy Spirit; whom he has abundantly poured out upon us through Jesus Christ, in order that, justified by his grace, we may be heirs in the hope of life everlasting" (Tt 3:4-7). In the above verses, St. Paul shows clearly the role of the Holy Spirit in our renewal and divinization.

This role will appear more vividly in the comparison of the seal, used by the Greek Fathers frequently. They got it from St. Paul, who wrote thus to the Ephesians: "It is in Christ Jesus that, when you heard the good news of your salvation, you believed and were sealed with the Holy Spirit, who was promised to you" (Ep 1:13). And to the Corinthians he wrote: "It is God who is warrant for us and for you in Christ, who has anointed us, who has also stamped us with his seal and has given us the Spirit as a pledge in our hearts" (2 Cor 1:21-22).

The seal represents the Holy Spirit. The imprint is that of the Son, but also of the Father, since the Son is the image of the Father. Consequently, the Holy Spirit is like the seal which bears the image of the Father and the Son, and which imprints this image in us. How? by his presence, for he is the image of the Son as the Son is the image of the Father. "The spotless image of the Father," writes St. Cyril of

Alexandria, "is the Son; the natural likeness of the Son, is his Spirit. That is why, refashioning human souls according to the divine likeness, he strikes on them the divine form and imprints on them the mark of the subatance which is above every substance" (*In Joan Evang.*). "When to show the great benefit that comes to us in being united to him," St. Cyril writes on another occasion, "Christ calls himself the true vine—he compares to its branches those who, united to him, are as grafted to him and are already partakers of his own nature, by receiving the Holy Spirit. For he who unites us to Christ the Savior is his Holy Spirit. . . If it is uniquely through the Spirit that Christ is formed in us, and he imprints there in some way his own traits, thus making live again in human nature the beauty of the Godhead, then the Spirit of Christ is really God" (*In Joan: Thesaurus*).

Elsewhere, the same Doctor of the Church, writes:

> *If it is true that we are remade according to the image of God by receiving the seal of the Holy Spirit, how can anyone assert that he is a creature, he through whom the image of the divine essence is imprinted in us, and the traits of the uncreated nature are represented in us? For the Holy Spirit does not work in us in the way a painter would who, a stranger to the divine essence, would reproduce its traits. It is not that way that the Holy Spirit restores the divine image in us. Being God, and proceeding from God, the Spirit imprints himself invisibly, like a seal upon wax, in the hearts of those who receive him. Thus through the communication that he makes of himself, he restores to our nature its original beauty, and re-makes man, according to the likeness of God. How can one say that the Holy Spirit is a creature, he through whom the human nature is re-fashioned in the image and likeness of God? (Thesaurus)*

The Holy Spirit is like the seal that carries the image of the Son, who is the image of the Father, and that imprints it in our souls as if on soft wax, by imprinting himself,—he who is himself the image of the Son.

However, the image carried on the seal is one thing, another is the image imprinted on the wax. Thus, the Fathers distinguish the divine nature, whose imprint is marked in the soul, and the impression produced, which really transforms the nature of the soul, and which we call *habitual grace,* or sanctifying, divinizing, or created grace. But they maintain that this impression is imprinted and maintained in the soul through the intimate presence in the soul of God himself—a presence called uncreated grace.

Since it is the Holy Spirit who imprints in our soul the image of God by imprinting himself, it is he who transforms us by making us similar to God, and who, in and by the same fact, makes the Father and the Son dwell in us, in an intimate and permanent manner, without intermediary other than their imprint, as the sun is present in the mirror without intermediary other than its image. "If anyone love me," Jesus said, "he will keep my word, and my Father will love him, and we will come and make our abode with him" (Jn 14:23).

The presence of the Holy Spirit in the Christian, is attributed to the Holy Spirit by Scripture. The reason for this attribution will make us understand yet better the capital role that the Holy Spirit plays in the work of our divinization.

The presence in us of the three divine Persons, which brings about our divinization, as we have seen, consists in our real union with them, through our participation in their life of knowledge and love. Now this participation in the divine life is appropriated to the Holy Spirit.

What is an appropriation? We know that all actions that God accomplishes to the exterior of himself, both in the natural order, like the creation of the world, and in the supernatural order, like Redemption, are common to the three divine Persons of the Holy Trinity, since the divine faculties from which these actions proceed are common to the three, except the passive Incarnation, i.e., the act by which the Word incarnated himself—an act which is proper to the Son only. Nevertheless, some of these actions—like certain divine names—are attributed to a determined divine Person. We call these attributions appropriations.

An appropriation flows from the affinity between a certain action and the specific character of the Person to whom it is attributed. Thus in the *Creed* we attribute to the Father the works of power, as the creation of the world, because he is the source of Being. To the Son we attribute the work of our salvation, because being the

Word of God, the exact image of the Father, he remakes us according to the image of the Father and the Son, thanks to his redemptive work. To the Holy Spirit, we attribute the works of love, like the union of the Word with human nature, like also precisely our participation in the divine life.

To be sure, it is God the Father who, "possessing life in himself," as St. John says (Jn 5:26), communicates to us this life in his Son, Jesus Christ, "to whom the Father has given to have life in himself," and who has merited for us to possess this life ourselves. Nevertheless, he communicates this life through the Holy Spirit. It is the Holy Spirit who, because he is Love personified and because love is the principle of union, unites us to Christ dead and resurrected, hence to his glorified humanity. He thus vivifies us with the divine life, being the breath of love of the Father and the Son. That is why, though our participation in the life of God, and thus to his nature, is the work common to the three divine Persons, it is appropriated, attributed to the Holy Spirit.

It devolves upon the Holy Spirit to realize our union with the glorious Christ. Because he is the Spirit of truth, the Holy Spirit has for his mission to instruct us with the whole truth, revealed by Christ. He has for his mission, particularly, to impart to us a loving knowledge of the Father and the Son: a savoring knowledge, or an experience of love. In this participation consists our divine life. He is then the principle of our spiritual life: he is the life of our spirit which is vivified by the Spirit. Thus St. Paul could say: "We live by the Spirit" (Gal 5:25). And in the Creed we say: "We believe in the Holy Spirit, the Lord, the giver of life."

He gives us this life by infusing in us the theological virtues of faith, hope and charity, supernatural dispositions which enable us to know and love God, with the same knowledge and love with which the divine Persons love one another. In fact, St. Paul writes that it is the Spirit who infuses the faith in us: "No one can say 'Jesus is Lord' (i.e., God), except in the Holy Spirit" (1 Cor 12:3). It is the Spirit who infuses hope in us: "May the God of hope fill you with all joy and peace in believing, that you may abound in hope by the power of the Spirit" (Rm 15:13). Lastly, the Holy Spirit infuses charity in us: "The love of God is poured forth in our hearts by the Holy Spirit who has been given to us" (Rm 5:5).

There is yet another reason for attributing to the Holy Spirit the deifying presence of the Holy Trinity. Being the gift of the Father and the Son, the Spirit is the Person through whom the other two Persons communicate with us. It was fitting that he come first in us to make of us the temple of God. "In this we know that God abides in us," says St. Joyn, "by the Spirit whom he has given us" (1 Jn 3:24). It is through love that the lover gives himself to the beloved. "If anyone love me," Jesus said to his disciples, "my Father will love him (i.e., will give his Love who is the Spirit), and we will come and make our abode with him."

It remains for me to say a few words about the role of the Holy Spirit in the divinization of our body. It is the Holy Spirit, St. Paul says, who has resurrected the body of Christ; it will be he who will resurrect ours. "If the Spirit of him who raised Jesus from the dead dwells in you, then he who raised Jesus Christ from the dead will also bring to life your mortal bodies because of his Spirit who dwells in you" (Rm 8:11). Our body then will be a "spiritual body," namely, wholly penetrated and transformed by him, who St. Peter calls, "the Spirit of glory" (1 P 4:14). Our vital principle will no longer be the animal soul, subject to corruption and death: the *psyche*. It will become a spiritual principle, by participating in the Holy Spirit who will change it in *pneuma,* free from corruption and death. The Holy Spirit will communicate to our body his proper vitality and will transform it by impressing his form; he will spiritualize it by making it share his incorruptibility and immortality.

Waiting for that glorious event, though our body remains subject, here on earth, to corruption and death, the Holy Spirit deposits in it the seed of the glorious resurrection, by making it the temple of God. Moreover, he sanctifies it. "Holy is the temple of God, and this temple are you" (1 Cor 3:17); and in another place, St. Paul writes: "Do you not know that your members are the temple of the Holy Spirit, who is in you, whom you have from God, and that you are not your own?. . . Glorify then God in your body" (1 Cor 6:19-20).

In one of his sermons on the Nativity of our Lord St. Leo the Great cries out: "Let us give thanks to God through his Son and in the Holy Spirit, that having loved us in his infinite love, he has had pity for us. And as we were dead because of our sins, he has vivified us in Jesus Christ, so that we can be in him a new creature, a new work. Let us cast off then the old man and his works; let us renounce the works of the flesh. Recognize, O Christian, your dignity and having become a partaker of the divine nature, beware of falling back in the first baseness by a conduct not becoming to your grandeur. Recall of what head and body you are a member. And never forget that, having been snatched from the power of darkness, you have been translated to the light and kingdom of God" (Sermon 1 on the *Nativity of our Lord*).

CHAPTER SEVEN

The Holy Spirit, Principle of Our Filial Life

Dwelling in us, the Holy Spirit makes us partakers of the divine nature; he defies us by making us communicate in the nature of the Persons of the Trinity. This participation, as we are going to see, is realized through the communion of love which the Holy Spirit establishes between the Word of God become flesh and us. Our communion, St. John tells us, is not only with the Father but also with his Son, Jesus Christ (cf. 1 Jn 1:4). And St. Paul writes: "God is trustworthy who has called us into fellowship with his Son, Jesus Christ our Lord" (1 Cor 1:9).

We have seen that the Holy Spirit makes us partakers of the divine nature through its impression that he imprints in our soul. Now, the impression is of the nature as possessed by the God-Man, Jesus Christ. The Fathers of the Church, especially the Eastern Fathers, stress repeatedly the doctrine that the image of God—according to which God made man at the beginning and which he restored to him when the "fullness of time" had arrived—is the image of the Son. St. Irenaeus, for instance, goes so far as to say that our bodily nature itself was created according to the image of the God-Man, and was present in God's mind as such, when he created the first man. And St. Athanasius writes:

> *It was necessary that what had once partaken of the image of God did not perish. What was then God to do? Nothing less than to renew this image once imprinted in man, so that men could again through it know God. But how could that be done if not by the coming of the very Image of God, our Savior Jesus Christ? Indeed, that could not be done by men,*

*since they are (not images), but are (made) according to the
likeness (image) of God; nor could that be done by the
angels, for they too are not images (of God). That is why the
Word of God himself has come in the world in order that, as
the Image of the Father, he could renew man, made
according to the likenss of God* (De incar. Verbi).

Nature of Our Filial Life

Remade thus according to the image of God through our
communion with his Son Jesus Christ, we too become sons: "sons in
the Son," according to the strong expression of Emile Mersch, S. J.
"The Word became flesh," St. Irenaeus says, "the eternal Son of the
living God became the Son of Man in order that men might enter into
communion with the Word and by receiving the adoption, might
become sons of God."

The sacred writers speak often of our divine filiation through our
union with the unique Son. "You are all children of God," St. Paul
told the Galatians, "through faith in Jesus Christ. For all you have
been baptized into Christ, have put on Christ" (Gal 3:26-27). St. John
says: "To as many who received him (the Son of God become man),
he gave the power of becoming sons of God" (Jn 1:12).

The Fathers are inexhaustible on this subject. Their teaching is
summed in the concise phrase, "The Son of God became man in order
that men can become sons of God." To quote one text. St. Cyril of
Alexandria wrote:

*From the fact that they have received the Son by faith, men
receive the power to be reckoned in the number of sons of
God. For the Son makes man to be that which belongs only
to him by nature. He shares this power with men, loving
them. We could not otherwise avoid corruption, we who
carry with us the terrestrial image (of Adam), if we had not
been marked by the beauty of this celestial image (our
Savior) through the call to divine filiation. Having become
partakers of him through the Spirit, we are stamped
according to his likeness (image). . . Thus we are elevated to*

> *the supernatural dignity by Christ, but it is not by the same title which is his that we too are sons of God, but according to his image through grace* (In Joann. Evang.).

Therefore, we are made sons of God through our participation in the filiation of Christ. It is an adopted filiation, however, as St. Paul tells us: "When the fullness of time came, God sent his Son, born of a woman . . . that we might receive the adoption of sons" (Gal 4:4-5). "Blessed be the God and Father of our Lord Jesus Christ, who has belessed us with every spiritual blessings on high in Christ. . . He predestined us to be adopted through Jesus Christ as his sons" (Ep 1:3-6).

When a child is adopted in a family, he becomes a member of that family. He is treated exactly like the other members; he receives the same care, the same affection, and later the same heritage. Whatever may have been his original background, he is treated by the new parents as their own child, by the other children as their little brother or sister. It is the same with us, from the moment we receive the grace of Baptism and of faith, "we are no longer strangers and foreigners," as St. Paul says, "but citizens with the saints and members of God's household" (Ep 2:19).

Our filiation is one of grace—an adoptive filiation. Only Christ is Son by nature. To him only the Father communicates in fullness the divine nature, which becomes the Son's own nature. Accordingly, St. Athanasius wrote: "Through our origins and according to our nature, we are creatures. Later, we are adopted as sons; and then our Creator becomes also our Father. We are not sons by nature, but the Son, who is in us, is. God is not our Father by nature, but he is the Father of the Word, who is in us. In him and because of him, we cry, "*Abba,* Father!" That is why, as St. Cyril says, "all filiation comes through the son, because he only is really Son." Indeed, in him dwells the fullness of divinity; we are and remain creatures; hence, our filiation is an adoptive filiation.

However, the notion of adoption fails to convey adequately the reality of our filiation to the Father. Divine adoption is much more, by far, than human or legal adoption. Indeed, it is of another order completely. The relations established between an adopted child and his new parents, however loving and concerned they many be, are a juridical convention. For the legal adoption does not change the (physicical and bilogical) nature of the adopted child. It dos not instil into him the blood of his new parents. It does not make him a new being. The child remains what he was before his adoption, notwithstanding all the love and care with which he is surrounded.

Through the divine adoption, the Father makes us participate in the natural filiation of his only Son. Since the divine nature, (of which the Holy Spirit imprints the likeness in us) is possessed by the Son become man, Jesus Christ, a union is established between him and us—the closest union that can be imagined after the personal union of the Son with the human nature taken by him in the womb of the Virgin Mary. Our union with Christ is much more intimate than the natural union of our body and soul. It is a "physical" union, in the Greek sense of the word, namely, an essential and *ontological* union.

Our union with Christ is a union by identification to his being and his life. Between him and the Christian there is a community of being. According to the favorite expression of St. Paul, the Christian is "in Christ;" the Christian exists "in Christ;" he becomes "one same being with him." Emile Mersch, S.J., points out that, *en Xristw,* "in Christ," is used by St. Paul some 164 times in the few writings of his which remain. "The expression," writes Mersch, "must have been on his lips every moment, as the precept of love is on the lips of St. John" (*Le Corps Mystique du Christ.* Vol 1, p. 131).

The expression "in Christ," goes on to say Mersch, "is not only most frequent under St. Paul's pen; but is is also used in the most different contexts. The whole Church is 'in Christ,' the various individual churches are also 'in Christ.' Like their church, the faithful are 'in Christ;' they live 'in him;' they are holy 'in him;' 'in him' they have their virtues, their qualities, their functions, their sufferings, their joys, their glory. They walk 'in Christ,' in the strength and the grace given them 'in him;' they walk in the faith, hope and charity, which are 'in him,' to salvation, redemption, and renewal, which are 'in him.' "From God you are *in Christ Jesus,* who has become for us God-given wisdom, and justice and sanctification, and redemption" (1 Cor 1:30). And one can repeat and say it again, that they are born, that they live, that they work, that they die, *ab uno eodemque Christo non recedimus,* we never come out of Christ" (Mersch, op. cit. pp.133f).

Christ and the Christian form one and the same Christ, but in two persons. However, though this union does not do away with personal distinction, the identification with Christ is very real since it is a community of being, also a community of life. Because he is "in Christ," the Christian lives the life of Christ. Every Christian can say with St. Paul: "It is now no longer I that live, but Christ lives in me" (Gal 2:20).

This astonishing Pauline doctrine was what our Lord himself taught. "He who eats my flesh and drinks my blood," he said to the Jewish crowd at Jerusalem, "*abides in me* and *I in him. As the living Father has sent me, and as I live because of the Father, so he who eats me, he also shall live because of me*" (Jn 6:57-58). And at the vigil of his redemptive death, he told his disciples: "I will not leave you orphans; I will come to you. Yet a little while and the world no longer sees me. But you see me, for I live and you shall live. In that day you will know that I am in my Father, *and you in me;* and *I in you*" (Jn 14:18-21). Our Lord then compared our union with him with the union that exists between the Father and him, as stands out from his prayer to his Father at the Last Supper: "I pray also for those who will believe in me, that *all may be one, even as thou, Father, in me and I in thee;* that *they also may be one in us*" (Jn 17:20-21).

Such is the full reality of our divine adoption. It is an effective reality involving the transformatin of our being and the communication of a new life, thanks to the rebirth "of water and the Spirit," a "birth from on high," a "birth from God." As St. John says, our Lord "has given the power of becoming sons of God to those who believe in his name; who were born not of blood, nor of the will of the flesh, nor of the will of man, but of God" (Jn 1:12-13). A most convincing proof of his love. "Behold what manner of love the Father has bestowed upon us," exclaims St. John, "that we should be called children of God; and such we are," (1 Jn 3:2).

Thus our divine filiation is so real that we can consider it as a certain participation in the eternal birth of the Son in the bosom of the Father. "Consider our Lord," writes Origen; "the Father generates him perpetually. It is the same with the Christian faithful. The Savior is the "radiance of the Father's glory," and this radiance never ceases to be generated (radiated). If then the Savior is perpetually being generated by the Father, the same with us, if we

have the spirit of the filial adoption; God generates us perpetually in
him . . . his sons in Christ Jesus" (*Hom. IX in Jeremiam*).

The Role of the Spirit in Our Filial Life

Now, it is the Holy Spirit who engenders us as sons of God in his Son,
who makes us participate in the sonship of Christ, in his filial life.
"Whoever are led by the Spirit of God," St. Paul tells the Romans,"
they are the sons of God. Now you have not received a spirit of
bondage so as to be again in fear, but you have received a spirit of
adoption as sons, by virtue of which we cry, 'Abba! Father!' The
Spirit himself gives testimony to our spirit that we are sons of God.
But if we are sons, we are heirs also; heirs indeed of God and joint
heirs with Christ" (Rm 8:14-17).

The Father generates us by giving us a participation in the nature
of his Son. But as it was by the Holy Spirit that the Father realized the
conception of Jesus in the womb of Mary, so it is through the Holy
Spirit who engenders in us the life of children. So we can maintain
that we are generated equally by the Spirit. Our Lord said so: "Amen,
amen, I say to thee," he said to Nicodemus, "unless a man be born
again of water and the Spirit, he cannot enter into the kingdom of
God. That which is born of the flesh is flesh; and that which is born of
the Spirit is spirit. Do not wonder that I said to thee, 'You must be
born again.' The wind blows where it will, and thou hearest its sound
but dost not know where it comes from or where it goes. So is
everyone who is born of the Spirit" (Jn 3:5-8).

The Father generates us by making us conceive his Word in our
heart through the Holy Spirit, as he made the Word to be conceived
in Mary's womb through the action of the same Spirit. Our birth as
sons proceeds from a kind of conception in us of the Son of God.
"You have been reborn," writes St. Peter, "not from corruptible seed
but from incorruptible, through the word of God who lives and
abides forever" (1 P 1:23). St. John too speaks of a "seed of God" (cf.
1 Jn 3:9). After the Word of God united with an individual human
nature in the womb of Mary, through the hypostatic union, he
continues to unite, in the bosom of the Church, through the medium
of his glorified human nature, with a multitude of human natures—a

very real union though an infinitely less intimate one. "My dear children," St. Paul wrote to the Galatians, "with whom I am in labor again, until Christ is formed in you" (Gal 4:19).

This doctrine, which the primitive Christians expressed by saying that the Christian is a *Christophoros,* a Christ-bearer, has always been taught by the Church. The author of the Epistle to Diognetus, in the 2nd century, speaks of the Word sent to us by the Father, "who was from the beginning, who has appeared anew and has been recognized as ancient, and who, always new, is engendered in the heart of the saints." A century later, St. Ambrose will write: "If Christ has only one mother according to the flesh, he is the fruit of everyone according to the faith, for every soul can receive the Word of God, provided that the soul be pure and free of sins." Commenting on the answer of our Lord to the woman who cried, "Blessed be the womb that bore you and the breasts that nursed you," an answer that, as we know, goes this way: "Rather blessed are they who hear the Word of God and keep it." St. Bede the Venerable (675-735) writes: "The Savior declares the happiness not only of her who merited to generate corporally the Word of God, but also of all those who strive to conceive spiritually the same Word in the docility of their faith; and to make him to be born (again), and so to say, to nourish him in their hearts or in the hearts of their neighbors by a diligent practice of the good."

Blessed John of Avila writes to a religious: "Jesus will be born of you, since he said that whoever does the will of his Father who is in heaven will be his brother, his sister and his mother. The soul conceives him by love." And John Tauler makes our Lord say to a devout person: "I descend in your heart to be engendered in an ineffable manner by my Father." In this same work, he writes: "God, the eternal Father, will accomplish in us, unceasingly his eternal generation. Yes, I tell you, the generation of his eternal Word that he accomplishes in his eternity, he will accomplish it here on earth, as he does in heaven, neither more nor less" (*Institutions).*

And in our time, Paul Claudel has expressed strongly this truth in his *"L'epee et le miroir":* He writes: "It is not enough to esteem God with all the power of our intelligence, our soul and our body. It is not enough to reflect on him, it is not enough to welcome him, we must reproduce him: we must conceive him and engender him. We cannot receive Christ and remain ourselves. We must come to an agreement with this new principle of life which was introduced in us. We must furnish matter and substance to this seed which has been inserted in us. Like the Virgin gave birth to Christ, we must do the saame. We must strive to give form and a visage to *this principle in us who speaks to us,* so that the Word may become flesh once more, in us."

This conception of Christ in us is also the work of the Holy Spirit. It is of the Holy Spirit, as it was in the womb of Mary, that Christ is conceived in us. His action in us has formed the continuation of the work he accomplished in Mary. It is he who produced the body, the blood and the soul of Jesus Christ; it is he who produces mystically Jesus Christ in each of us. Our filiation in Christ, our generation as sons through the spiritual conception of Christ in us brought about by the Holy Spirit, is such that we are associated to the very act by which the Son, in the bosom of the Trinitarian life, breathes the Holy Spirit conjointly with the Father. We are identified with the Son of God become man in such a way, that the Spirit who proceeds from him and from the Father, proceeds also from us, at the same time and through the same event. "The Holy Spirit," says St. John of the Cross, "raises the soul most sublimely, and informs her, that she may breathe in God the same breath of love that the Father breathes in the Son and the Son in the Father, which is the same Holy Spirit that They breathe into her in the said transformation . . . It is to make us heirs to such an abyss of glory that God has created us to his image and likeness." In the Holy Trinity, wherein Christ has introduced us, we accomplish through participation the same work that he realizes through his nature, i.e., we breathe the Holy Spirit. And that is what Jesus was alluding to, when he declared: "He who believes in me, as the Scripture says, 'From within him there shall flow rivers of living water.' " And St. John explains that "he said this, however, of the Spirit whom they who believe in him were to receive" (Jn 7:37-39). Jesus had already told the Samaritan woman: "He who drinks of the water that I will give him shall never thirst; but the water that I will give him shall become in him a fountain of water, springing up into life everlasting" (Jn 4:14). The water of which Jesus speaks here symbolizes the Holy Spirit.

Of the role of the Holy Spirit in our divine adoption in the Son, Mersch writes thus: "There is only Son, but in this one the multitude of poor human sinners is taken up, and made in him sons, by an adoptive filiation, partakers of his natural filiation. The proof of this, St. Paul explains, is that they have in them the Spirit. God has saved them 'through the bath of regeneration and renewal by the Holy Spirit, whom he has abundantly poured out upon us through Jesus Christ our Savior' (Tt 3:5-6). Of this Spirit they are all full; he is given to them, he dwells in them, they are his temple, and the love of God is poured forth in their heart by this Spirit who has been given them. For them, the kingdom, this divine gift brought by Christ, is justice and peace and joy in the Holy Spirit" (Rm 14:17).

Mersch then adds:

> *The Holy Spirit is their interior principle of life, of strength, of love, of holiness, of joy; it is he who leads them, he who renews them, he who gives them the pledge of the resurrection and glory that awaits them, he who instils in them the appreciation and perception which is fitting to Christians; it is he who, at Baptism, unites them with Christ, he who stamped their soul with the seal of salvation, he who draws from their heart prayers which go straight to God, and make them cry to the Most High himself, Father.* (Mersch, *op. cit.*, vol. I, pp. 199 f.)

In faith we know the Father with the same knowledge with which Jesus knows his Father, and the Father knows the Son. "I am the good Shepherd," Jesus said, "and I know mine and mine know me, even as the Father knows me and I know the Father" (Jn 10:14). Now, Jesus knows his Father in the Image that he is of his Father. Consequnetly, we too know the Father in this same image, imprinted in us. We perceive in us the image of the Son and through it the image of the Father. "When the soul," says St. Athanasius, "thrusts aside from it every stain of sin, which covers it, and keeps only that which is pure and comformed to the image, when the image shines, it sees there as in a mirror the Word Image of the Father, and in him it represents to itself the features of the Father, of whom our Savior is the Image" (*Contra Gentes*). This follows from what we have learned about the mystery of the Holy Trinity, namely, that the Son is the perfect Image of the Father. He is his *alter ego,* hence, he is the exact and total revelation of the Father.

Christ is the Son of God himself living and acting in a human manner in the world. That is why to know him is to know the Father, as Jesus said to the Apostle Thomas: "If you had known me, you would also have known my Father. And henceforth you do know him and you have seen him" £Jn 14-7-10). And to Ptilip: "He who sees me sees also the Father. Do you not believe that I am in the Father and the Father is in me?" Through the existence of Christ, his way of thinking, willing and living, Rhrist makes us know the Father.

Since our filial life consists in knowing the Father with the same knowledge with which Christ knows him, it definitely consists in knowing Christ himself. People like us have seen and heard Jesus: they have written about his deeds and recorded his words and teachings, with the assistance of the Holy Spirit. Others illumined by the same Spirit have spoken about him before his advent in the world; others, finally, aided by the same Spirit, have spoken about him after his death, and have developed his teachings. The totality of these writings, which inform us about his person and doctrine, make up the Sacred Scriptures or the Bible.

In order to know Jesus Christ and, in him, the Father, we must read and meditate the Bible. With the aid of the Holy Spirit who, according to the promise of Jesus, must teach us all things, must recall to us the full message of Jesus, and must make us enter in the whole truth (cf. Jn 14:26; 16:13). That is why the Church makes us ask the Holy Spirit: "Grant that through you we may know the Father as well as the Son" (*Veni Creator*). "Reborn by Baptism," writes St. Irenaeus, "which is given to us in the name of the three divine Persons, we are enriched with goods which are in God the Father, through his Son, and the Holy Spirit. For, those who are baptized, or reborn, again, receive the Spirit of God, who has given them to the Word, and the Son takes them and offers them to his Father, and the Father confers upon them incorruptibility. Thus, without the Holy Spirit, we cannot see the Word of God; and without the Son no one can go to the Father, since the knowledge of the Father is the Son, and the knowledge of the Son is obtained through the Holy Spirit" (*Demonstration of the Apostolic Preaching*).

The Holy Spirit makes us know the Father and the Son, or more exactly, the Son and in the Son, the Father, because he (the Spirit) is Love, personal and substantial.

St. John says that "the Spirit is truth" (1 Jn 5:6). He is "truth" precisely because he proceeds from the Father and the Son, or because he is their love. Jesus too calls the Holy Spirit, "the Spirit of truth" (Jn 14:17). However, our Lord did not want to say that the Holy Spirit is the "truth," (as such), but that he (the Spirit) is his (Jesus') Spirit, who said: "I am the way, and the *truth,* and the life" (Jn 14:6). It is then because he is Love that the Holy Spirit makes the Father and the Son known.

Love has for its object the good. Because of this, it makes us seek, desire and know that which is good; hence, also and above all, the Absolute Good, which is God. Love is also intuitive and reaches its object from its interior (*intus),* what it is in itself. We see the essential role of the Spirit of Love in our knowledge of Christ and, in him, of the Father. Also we should understand the usage of the Church to invoke the light of the Holy Spirit to make our spirits perceive the truth. It is not because the Holy Spirit is himself the Truth, but because he is the Fire of Love, of the *Veni Creator.* Enkindling in us the fire of love, the Holy Spirit confers to the eyes of our intelligence the faculty to enable them to illuminate and scrutinize in depth what they look at. He also gives to our poor and feeble love the power to attain a supernatural understanding of divine truth, an experiential knowledge, since he makes us conform to it. He is all the more the Spirit of Truth, and as such, he is the substantial and living yearning for the perfect understanding of and conformity to the infinite Truth from whom he proceeds.

It is the Holy Spirit who also prepares men of all times and places to make the encounter with their Savior. The Spirit instills in hearts the yearning for the good, the true and the beautiful. He confers the capacity to seek and find Christ, by showing that the Savior only meets our deepest yearnings for completion and blessedness.

It is the Holy Spirit who also aids visibly those who make Jesus known. In fact, and we have already seen, in the primitive Church, the word and preaching of the messengers of Jesus "was a demonstration of the power of the Spirit" (1 Cor 2:4). The preaching of the good tidings was accompanied by "the works and power of the Holy Spirit:" their witness of Jesus was verified "by signs and wonders and by manifold powers and by impartings of the Holy Spirit" (Heb 2:3-4). It seems that what took place in the first days of the Church is happening again in our days!

It is against the Holy Spirit that one sins when he refuses willfully to recognize and accept Jesus Christ. It is the sin against the Holy Spirit, of which our Lord speaks: "Amen I say to you, that all sins shall be forgiven to the sons of men, and the blasphemies wherewith they blaspheme; but whoever blasphemes against the Holy Spirit never has forgiveness, but will be guilty of an everlasting sin" (Mk 3:28-29). St. Matthew more precisely says: "Therefore I say to you, that every kind of sin and blasphemy shall be forgiven to men; but the blasphemy against the Spirit will not be forgiven. And whoever speaks a word against the Son of Man, it shall be forgiven him; but whoever speaks against the Holy Spirit, it will not be forgiven him, either in this world or in the world to come" (Mt 12:31-32). Here, of course, there is no "condemnation without appeal," points out the Ecumenical Bible, "but a warning to be on one's guard in order not to be condemned." And the Jerusalem Bible explains thus this text: "Man may be excused if he is mistaken about the divine dignity of Jesus, veiled as he is by his humble appearance as the Son of Man. He is not excusable if he shuts his eyes and heart when confronted with the astoundng works done by Jesus in the Spirit. By denying them, he rejects the supreme offer that God does to him, and thus puts himself outside salvation."

The sin against the Holy Spirit then consists in denying the testimony of the Holy Spirit who works in Jesus' astounding works, and in spite of the light that he gives to make him known. By refusing this recognition, one opposes himself to the Holy Spirit and blasphemes against him. If one persists in this attitude up to the end, he will not be forgiven for then his refusal will be a rejection of the light of the Holy Spirit, lucidly and freely opposed to the end. However, we may wonder whether it is possible for one to lucidly and freely reject the light of the Holy Spirit, up to the end!

At the same time that he makes us know Jesus Christ, the Holy Spirit makes us love him. Love and knowledge are closely tied. Love flows from knowledge; we cannot love something unless we know about it in some way. The Holy Spirit makes us know Jesus Christ in order that we might love him, and he deepens this knowledge in us in the measure that we accept and love him. Moreover, we do not really know a person except when we love him. Then, love requires the stimulant of knowledge, for he who loves desires to know better the beloved in order to love him the more. To make us love Jesus more, the Holy Spirit makes him attractive to us. This attraction, however, must be a divine attraction. Only the Holy Spirit instils and develops this attraction, and makes us love Christ with a love which corresponds to his divine being, a love which is a participation in the love with which the Father loves him—and who is no other than the Holy Spirit himself. He introduces us into the depths of Christ's filial life, by making us communicate the knowledge that he has of his Father through the loving knowledge of the Son that the Spirit gives us.

The filial life does not consist only in the participation in the knowledge that our Lord has of his Father, but also of his love for him. We know that there is no more basic disposition in Christ than his love for his Father. He often expressed this filial love in words like the following: "The world must know that I love the Father" (Jn 14:31); and "I have kept my Father's commandments and I abide in his love" (Jn 15:10). He also used often the Aramean term, *Abba,* to address and to refer to his Father. This word means father but with a nuance of tenderness. Now every time that Jesus pronounced this word, it was under the impulse of the Holy Spirit. Having become adoptive in Jesus Christ, we too can love the Father as he does; we too, with Jesus and in him can call God: *Abba.* "You have received a Spirit of adoption as sons by virtue of which we cry, 'Abba! Father!' The Spirit himself gives testimony that we are sons of God" (Rm 8:15-16); and "Because you are sons, God has sent the Spirit of his Son into our heart, who cries, 'Abba! Father!' " (Gal 4:6).

St. Paul shows to what point the Holy Spirit has become the soul of our soul. On the other hand, to say in what way the Holy Spirit makes us pronounce the word "Abba," in order to make us express to the Father our filial love, he uses the verb "to cry." He could not have chosen a better term. In fact, the cry manifests the vehemence of our sentiments, whatever they may be. How better to express to the Father than in a cry, the love, the joy, the enthusiasm, the wonder, the tenderness, which the awareness of our marvellous dignity of sons, provokes in us.

We are here at the source of prayer. It has become a classic expression to call prayer a "respiration of the soul." St. Francis de Sales writes about prayer: "By it we inhale in God and exhale in him, and he breathes in us and exhales upon us!"

Prayer is to the spiritual life of the Christian what breathing is to the life of the body. "To pray," writes Kierkegaard, "is to breathe. If I do not pray, I die spiritually." Numerous Christians live without praying, they do not feel the need of praying, and if they pray, it is only a formalist and legalistic affair. The need to pray is situated on a supernatural plane. No one can say to God "Father," unless through the action of the Holy Spirit. Prayer is an exigency of faith, hope and charity.

There is a great similarity between prayer and breathing. The latter is the symbol of the first from the fact that the breath of air we inhale and exhale by breathing is the symbol of the Holy Spirit, to whom it has given his name. The word breath is translated in Latin by that of *spiritus*. Our Lord himself, we have seen, certified this symbol when, appearing to his disciples after his Resurrection, he breathed on them saying: "receive the Holy Spirit" (Jn 20:22).

Breathing involves first of all inhaling air. The air inhaled vivifies the whole body for, by filling the lungs, it spreads oxygen in the blood, which irrigates all bodily members, especially the brain. All the body, then, finds itself re-vitalized. Next, the air that one has inhaled is exhaled.

Likewise, to pray is, first of all, to inhale the Holy Spirit, i.e., the breath of love of the Father; it is to draw him into oneself, or more exactly, to welcome him. It is not I who by the movement of my chest draws the air into my lungs; it is not I who exerts an attraction on the air in which my being bathes. On the contrary, it is the air which presses on my lungs—it is the atmospheric pressure—which penetrates in them when I expand my breast.

When I pray it is not my soul which draws the Breath of Love of the Father, the Holy Spirit, but is is the Holy Spirit who fills the whole universe who presses on my heart, since he is the love with which the Father loves us and since the Father who has loved us from all eternity, "has loved us first" (1 Jn 4:9), I need to only open my heart to this Breath of Love, and welcome the love of the Father. Also when we invoke the Holy Spirit, saying, *"Veni, Creator Spiritus,"* or all the *"Veni"* of the *"Veni Sancte Spiritus."* we should understand better the meaning of the invocation. Our intention should not be to implore him to come. He asks for nothing else, he to whom can be applied the words of the Apocalypse: "I stand at the door and knock. If any man listens to my voice and opens the door to me, I will come in to him" (Rv 3:20). Our intention, in calling on the Spirit is to tell him that we are opening the door of our heart, that we accept his offer to love, and therefore he can come to us, or if he is already in us, he can take possession more and more of us.

Prayer, consequently, consists of receiving or inhaling the Holy Spirit, the Spirit of the Father, then in exhaling or giving him back to the Father, in filial love.

Interior prayer can be reduced to this inhaling and this exhaling, to this breathing of love. One could do it to the rhythm of the bodily breathing, preferably, in a sitting position. This way of praying helps to make our whole being, body and soul, participate in the prayer; and to make the body profit of the benefits received by the soul. This respiration will be deeper the more we are united with Christ, the well-beloved of the Father, for it will coincide with the breathing of Christ. From this flows the necessity to let the Holy Spirit make us know and love Christ in order to be identified with him more and more.

Now, the breathing of Christ consists in breathing the Breath of love in which the Father says to him: "You are my Son, today I have begotten you"; "You are my Son in whom I have placed all my love." Then exhale the same Breath of Love in which he recognizes himself Son and expresses his thankfulness of Son, saying to him: "Abba, well-beloved Father!"

Our breathing will imitate that of Christ; better, it will have to be based on it. It will, consequently, consist of breathing the Spirit, the Breath of love of the Father, listening the Father says to us; "You are my child in whom I have placed all my love; then, to exhale this same breath of love, as the Breath of love of the Son, in whom we recognize ourselves sons and we express our love of sons, crying to him: "Abba, well-beloved Father!"

This breathing of love can be expressed in different ways. Accordingly the different reactions that will provoke in us the words by which, in order to reveal his love, God reveals to us such or such aspect of his mystery, makes us see such and such of his perfections, or reminds us of such and such of his wondrous works of love, our breathing will express itself in the following ways:

To the thought of the transcendence of the Father, the Creator, our prayer will express itself in the love of adoration and glorification. Before one or the other of God's perfections seen in his creatures or manifested through his interventions in the history of man, such as his beauty, his holiness, his goodness, his mercy, his faithfulness, his tenderness, and so forth, our prayer will express itself in the love of praise, To the recollection of the wonders he has accomplished for the whole of mankind: Creation, Incarnation, Redemption, the Eucharist, and so forth; and the graces he has given to each of us, our prayer will express itself in the love of admiration, and thanksgiving. To the remembrance of our sins, our prayer will express itself in the love of repentance and contrition. And remembering also our needs and those of others, our prayer will express itself in the love of petition and intercession.

In this silent heart-to-heart where the Father engenders us, every moment, as sons in his Son, by his Breath of love, and he gives us, in his Son, rest, peace, joy, strength, light, purification, consolation and love, we can only repeat: "Father, well-beloved Father!"

Such is the final outcome of the mission of the Holy Spirit. He is sent in our heart to make of our existence a cry of love for the Father. From the depths of our heart where he dwells, he utters this filial cry, the human echo of the eternal cry of love of the Son to his Father, and he exerts himself to raise and carry along our heart in the same cry, that we may express our love to the Father with an ardor similar to that of his Son. By making us rejoin the Father by the Son, he leads our love to his supreme end, in the same movement of love which draws the Son towards the Father.

CHAPTER EIGHT

The Holy Spirit, Principle of Our Sacramental and Moral Life

Since the Holy Spirit is the principle of our divine life as sons of God, he also is the principle of the effectiveness of the means by which the divine life is communicated and maintained in us, mainly the Sacraments. And since our life as sons of God demands that we conform ourselves to divine morals, the Holy Spirit is also the principle of our moral life.

The Sacraments, as we know, are sensible signs which manifest the action of the Holy Spirit in the work of our divinization and our filial life.

Baptism. It would seem at first sight, that the Holy Spirit does not have a special role in the first of the seven Sacraments: *Baptism.* In fact, the Acts calls it "the baptism in the name of the Lord Jesus" (Ac 8:16; 19:5) or "baptism of Jesus Christ" (Ac 2:38; 10:48). Moreover, our Lord ordered his disciples to "baptize in the name of the Father, and of the Son, and of the Holy Spirit" (Mt. 28:19).

However, in the passages of the Acts, just cited, St. Luke uses the words "baptism of Jesus," to distinguish this baptism from that which he calls "the baptism of John" the Baptist. In fact, when St. Paul asked some converts at Ephesus, "How were you baptized, " they answered, "With John's baptism." Then St. Paul said to hem: "John baptized the people with a baptism of repentance, telling them to believe in him who was to come after him, that is, in Jesus. On hearing this they were baptized in the name of the Lord Jesus" (Ac 19:3-5). As for the expression "to baptize in the name of the Father, of the Son and of the Holy Spirit," it signifies that Baptism "plunges" (to baptize means to plunge) us into the Holy Trinity; it introduces us in the life of the three divine Persons.

Though it is a baptism in the name of Jesus and a baptism given in the name of the Persons of the Holy Trinity, Scripture maintains that this Sacrament is a baptism "in the Holy Spirit" (Mt 3:12; Mk 1:8; Lk 3:16). Our Lord himself calls it thus: "John indeed baptized with water, but you shall be baptized in the (with the) Holy Spirit not many days hence" (Ac 1:5). In his talk with Nicodemus, Jesus had spoken on the role of the Holy Spirit in the new birth that Baptism brings about. Jesus answered, "Amen, amen, I say to thee, unless a man be born again of water and the Spirit, he cannot enter into the kingdom of God. That which is born of the flesh is flesh; and that which is born of the Spirit is spirit" (Jn 3:5-6).

All these texts highlight the primordial role of the Holy Spirit in Baptism. This Sacrament brings about a true rebirth (regeneration); it frees us from spiritual death by deleting Original Sin, which is the cause of death; and it gives us divine life; it sanctifies and vivifies. It is logical that this sanctification and vivifying be attributed to the Holy Spirit, who is precisely the Sanctifier and Vivifier in person. Moreover, our re-birth in Baptism corresponds to the conception of Christ in the mystery of the Incarnation. Our rebirth in Baptism to divine life is consequently a work of love; therefore, a work of the Spirit, as was the conception of Jesus.

Confirmation. This Sacrament is the completion of Baptism, and has always been called the Sacrament of the Holy Spirit. Conferred on us to make us attain to the fullness of the spiritual life, its adult age; and to make of us witnesses of Christ, and with him the witnesses of Trinitarian love, Confirmation communicates to us love and strength, for this witnessing. It pertains to him, who is the Love and the Power of God, i.e., the Holy Spirit, to produce in us a strong and fearless love. He does that by conferring on the fullness of his gifts. That is what the prayers, which precede the anointing with chrism, express.

The bishop begins by saying to his assistants: "Let us ask of God our Father to send the Holy Spirit on these children to fill them with his gifts. Then, he says: "Let us ask for them that the Holy Spirit may act in the depths of their spirit and make them like Jesus Christ." Then, in a gesture which accompanies the prayer for the coming of the Spirit, the bishop and concelebrating priests extend their hands over all those to be confirmed. This expresses the biblical gesture by which the gift of the Holy Spirit is invoked. The bishop prays:

> *most loving and All-powerful God, Father of our Lord Jesus Christ, by water and the Holy Spirit you freed these candidates, your children, from sin. Send your Holy Spirit upon them by their Helper and Guide. Give them the spirit of wisdom and understanding, the spirit of right judgment and courage, the spirit of knowlege and love, the spirit of reverence in your service (We ask this) through Christ our Lord.*

Penance or Reconciliation. When Christ instituted the Sacrament of Penance or Reconciliation, he gave his disciples the power to remit sins. He did this by communicating to them, through his breath, the Holy Spirit, to remit sins. "Receive the Holy Spirit," he said to them; "whose sins you shall forgive, they are forgiven them; and whose sins you shall retain, they are retained" (Jn 20:22). In the same manner, the bishop transmits the power of confession to the priest he is ordaining. The liturgy calls the Holy Spirit "the remission of all sins." This expression appears in the new formula of absolution:

> *God, the Father of mercies, through the death and resurrection of his Son has reconciled the world to himself and sent the Holy Spirit among us for the forgiveness of sins; through the ministry of the Church may God give you pardon and peace, and I absolve you from your sins in the name of the Father, and of the Son, and of the Holy Spirit.*

Forgiveness is a work of love, the expression of the love that God grants to the repentant sinner. A gesture of love of the Father and the Son, it is fitting that the remission of sins be inspired by him who is their Spirit of Love. Each absolution washes the repentant sinner; it purifies him in the fire of the Spirit of love. This deed of forgiveness and reconciliation is expressed beautifully in a Prayer of Thanksgiving, in the new rite for this Sacrament:

Almighty and merciful God, how wonderful you created man and still more wonderfully remade him. You do not abandon the sinner but seek him out with a father's love. You sent your Son in the world to destroy sin and death by his passion, and to restore life and joy by his resurrection. You sent the Holy Spirit into our hearts to make us your children and heirs of your kingdom. You constantly renew our spirit in the sacrament of your redeeming love, freeing us more into the likeness of your beloved Son. We thank you for the wonders of your mercy, and with heart and hand and voice we join with the whole Church in a new song of praise: Glory to you, through Christ in the Holy Spirit, now and forever.

The Eucharist. The role of the Holy Spirit in the Sacrament of the Eucharist does not appear at first sight. Isn't the Eucharist essentially the Sacrament of the Body and Blood of Christ!? Yet, examining this Sacrament more closely, we soon discover the role of the Holy Spirit in its three aspects: the Sacrifice, the Real Presence, and Communion.

In the Sacrifice. The Mass makes sacramentally present, thanks to the bread and wine changed into the Body and Blood of Jesus Christ, the sacrifice of the Cross, through the Last Supper. Now, we have seen that it was under the impulse of the Holy Spirit that Christ went to Calvary. The Epistle to Hebrews speaks of the blood of Christ "who, through the Holy Spirit offered himself unblemished unto God" (Heb 9:14). It was also under the impulse of the Holy Spirit that our Lord celebrated the Last Supper. The sacrifice of the Last Supper is, like the Mass, the same sacrifice of the Cross, because it was an anticipated sacramental representation. The same Spirit who drove Christ to offer himself to God, on the Cross, must have driven him to anticipate his bloody offering in the offering of his Flesh and Blood under the signs of bread and wine.

In the Real Presence. The Holy Spirit acts equally in effecting the real presence, which, as the Church teaches, is the transsubstantiation of the bread and wine into the Body and Blood of Jesus Christ. This happens through the words of Christ: "This is my Body; This is my Blood." But it is through the power of the Holy

Spirit that the consecratory words act on the bread and wine to change them. The new Eucharistic prayers highlight this role of the Holy Spirit, thanks to the insertion in the text of what we call the *epiclese,* namely, the invocation of the Holy Spirit on the offerings: the bread and the wine, through which the celebrant asks the Father to accomplish the transformation through his Holy Spirit.

Here are the texts of the *epiclese:*

> *Lord, you are holy indeed, the fountain of all holiness. Let your Spirit come upon these gifts to make them holy, so that they may become for us the body and blood of our Lord Jesus Christ.* (Eucharistic prayer II)

> *And so, Father, we bring you these gifts. We ask yo to make them holy by the power of your Spirit, that they may become the body and blood of your Son, our Lord Jesus Christ, at whose command we celebrate this Eucharist.* (Eucharistic Prayer III)

> *Father, may this Holy Spirit sanctify these offerings. Let them become the body and blood of Jesus Christ our Lord as we celebrate the great mystery which he left us as an everlasting covenant.* (Eucharistic Prayer IV)

The Liturgy attributes to the Holy Spirit the efficacy of the consecratory words of Christ, because the change of the bread and the wine into the Body and Blood of Christ is a deed so extraordinary that it requires the intervention of the divine power; hence, the intervention of the Holy Spirit, who is God's Power personified. That is why, the priest introduces the *epiclese* of the 3d Eucharistic Prayer, by saying: "Father. . . we ask to make these gifts holy by the power of your Spirit."

Communion. The Holy Spirit plays a primordial role in the Eucharistic Communion.

It is through the Holy Spirit that the Eucharistic Body of Christ nourishes him who eats it. "It is the Spirit that gives life; the flesh profits nothing," our Lord said about this nourishment (Jn 6:62-63).

It is the Spirit who, according to St. Paul, transformed Christ, the day of his Resurrection, into a "lifegiving Spirit," by spiritualizing his natural body, through the transformation of its vital principle into a spiritual principle. He gave him the possibility of being present in us and to make us live of his divine life, which the Eucharistic Communion develops in us, as our Lord once said: "He who eats my flesh and drinks my blood has life everlasting and I will raise him up on the last day. For my flesh is food indeed, and my blood is drink indeed. He who eats my flesh and drinks my blood, abides in me and I in him" (Jn 6:55-57). Now, it is the Holy Spirit, as we have seen who, through Christ, being present in us in Baptism, communicates this life. It is also he who develops it in us by the sacramental Communion, increasing our faith and our love. Thus, St. Paul calls the Eucharist a "spiritual food" and a "spiritual drink" (1 Cor 10:1-4): and says that "we have been baptized in one Spirit . . . and we were all given to drink of one Spirit" (1 Cor 12:13).

The Holy Spirit also makes the Communion produce its final goal, that of changing in Jesus Christ the faithful who receive the Eucharist: to sanctify them. This role belongs to the Holy Spirit, the Sanctifier. This action of the Spirit is highlighted in the new Eucharistic prayers, thanks to the second *epiclese*. The faithful ask the Holy Spirit to accomplish in them the work that he began on the day of Pentecost, which is precisely to sanctify them and to unite them to Jesus Christ, and in Jesus Christ make of them his Body.

Here is what these new prayers make the faithful ask of the Father:

> *May all of us who share in the body and*
> *blood of Christ*
> *be brought together in unity by the*
> *Holy Spirit.* (Eucharistic Prayer II)

> *Grant that we, who are nourished by his*
> *body and blood*
> *may be filled with his Holy Spirit*
> *and become one body, one spirit*
> *in Christ.* (Eucharistic Prayer III)

> *Lord, look upon this sacrifice which you*
> *   have given to your Church;*
> *and by your Holy Spirit, gather all who*
> *   share this bread and wine*
> *into the one Body of Christ, a living*
> *   sacrifice of praise.* (Eucharistic Prayer IV)

As we can see, there is a double *epiclese*: an invocation of the Holy Spirit on the gifts to consecrate, so that they become the Body and the Blood of Jesus Christ, and an invocation on the communicants themselves, that they may form one body, in drawing from the Communion an increase of fraternal love. Thus, after consecration, the celebrant addresses to God this prayer:

> *Lord, remember your Church throughout*
> *   the world:*
> *make us grow in love.* (Eucharistic Prayer II)

Holy Orders. The Holy Spirit also intervenes in the Sacrament of Orders. Two texts of St. Paul show this. In the first letter to his disciple, Timothy, the Apostle writes: "Do not neglect that grace that is in thee, granted to thee by reason of prophecy with the laying on of hands of the presbyterate" (1 Tm 4:14). And in the second letter, Paul writes: "I admonish thee to stir up the grace of God which is in thee by the laying on of my hands. For God has not given us the Spirit of fear, but a Spirit of power and of love and of prudence" (2 Tm 1:6-7). From the Acts, we can see that the gift mentioned in the two preceding texts—the gift conferred by the imposition on of hands—indicates the anointment of the Holy Spirit with which God marks the priest, and by which he consecrates him and sets him aside for his service, clothing him with power of his Spirit for the mission entrusted to him:

> *As they were ministering to the Lord and fasting, the Holy Spirit said, 'Set apart for me Saul and Barnabas unto the work to which I have called them.' Then, having fasted and prayed and laid their hands upon them, they so let them go. So they, sent forth the Holy Spirit, went to Seleucia and from there sailed to Cyprus (Ac 13:2-4).*

The Sacrament of Orders makes of a man a mediator between God and men. Such is the meaning of the priesthood. One can apply to the Christian priest the definition of the high priest of the Levitical priesthood: "Every high priest," says the author of Hebrews, "taken from among men is appointed for men in the things pertaining to God, that he may offer gifts and sacrifice for sins" (Heb 5:1). "There is one Mediator," St. Paul says, "between God and men, himself man, Christ Jesus" (1 Tm 2:5). The priest is a mediator between God and men in the sense that he is the minister of the mediation of the only sovereign Priest, Jesus Christ. However, this does not prevent the priest from representing the Christ-Priest in the strong sense of the term, namely, that the human priest makes Christ really present, so much so, that when he exercises his sacred functions, he acts in the person of Christ. His words and actions are the words and actions of Christ. When he pronounces the words of consecration, when he baptizes, when he forgives sin, it is Christ who consecrates, who baptizes, who forgives sins. He is the visible sign, the living sacrament of Christ. He makes Christ sacramentally, but really, present. The Sacrament of Orders then, conforms the priest to the Christ-Priest. This extraordinary deed presupposes the intervention of the power of the Holy Spirit.

Conformed to the Christ-Priest, the ordained is, like Him, the anointed of the Holy Spirit, and is thus consecrated for God and set aside for his service to accomplish the mission assigned to him, a mission which is the continuation of that of Christ. This mission, consists in announcing and communicating to men the love of God. It presupposes also the intervention of the Holy Spirit, for it is through him that God communicates his love: "The love of God," says St. Paul, "is poured forth in our hearts by the Holy Spirit who has been given to us" (Rm 5:5). The Sacrament of Orders confers to the priest the necessary powers for the accomplishment of his mission: the power to sanctify, to give men the divine life through the Sacraments; the power to teach them the truths of the faith; and the power to direct them in the Christian life. All these powers are meant to spread Love among men. Priests are, consequently, in the service of the Holy Spirit. It is he who, through the priest, sanctifies, teaches and directs.

The exercise of these powers demands the intervention of the

Holy Spirit, insofar as he is the power of God personified.

The power to administer the Sacraments permits the priest to make of man a god, to communicate to him divine life, to change the bread and the wine into the Body and Blood of Christ, to forgive sins, to heal the sick. Such an extraordinary power requires the power of the Holy Spirit.

The power to teach demands the power of the Spirit. The priest must "announce the word of God in all boldness" (Ac 4:29); his word must not be "a human word but really the word of God" (1 Tm 2:13); the faith must not "rest on the wisdom of men, but on the power of God" (1 Cor 2:5). That is why, the preaching of the Gospel, according to St. Paul, is "a demonstration of the power of the Spirit" (1 Cor 2:4). Moreover, in order to keep the faith intact, the priest needs the aid of the Holy Spirit who is the "Spirit of truth," and whose mission is, to again recall the words of Jesus, "to teach us all things, to bring to our minds whatever I have said" (Jn 14:26). Thus St. Paul wrote to his disciple Timothy: "Guard the good trust (the revealed truths) through the Holy Spirit, who dwells in us" (2 Tm 2:14).

Regarding a third power, which consists in leading the faithful in the ways of love, the priest exercises this power with the assistance of the Holy Spirit: the Spirit of Love. Accordingly, St. Paul said to the presbyters of the Church at Ephesus: "Take heed to yourselves and to the whole flock in which the Holy Spirit has placed bishops, to rule the Church of God, which he has purchased with his own blood" (Ac 20:28).

Finally, because of the exigencies of this priestly character and of the sacred functions with which the Sacrament of Orders charges him, the priest must be "for the faithful an example in speech, in conduct, in love, in faith, in chastity" (1 Tm 4:12). Thus more than any of the faithful, the priest has need of the Holy Spirit.

Marriage. In the Sacrament of Marriage, because he is the Spirit of Love, the Holy Spirit intervenes to transform by his power, human love, to give it a divine dimension. The Holy Spirit unites the spouses in Christ. He gives them the strength to make of their union one of permanent love, similar to the union that binds the Father and the Son, and a fecund union—the Spirit being himself the unceasing outpouring of divine love.

The Anointing of the Sick. Again because he is love and strength the Holy Spirit intervenes and makes efficacious the Sacrament of the Sick. This Sacrament has for its end to aid the sick to struggle against sickness and suffering, to heal them, and to sustain the sick in their last fight, which precedes their passage from this life to the other. The sick person needs special strength to make of his last breath a breath of love. By the anointing with the oil of the sick, the Holy Spirit communicates to the sick person strength and love.

The action which the Holy Spirit exerts in this Sacrament is shown in the words which conclude the rite: "N., the Holy Spirit has done great things in you. Henceforth, the strength of God works in your weakness." And when the priest prays to God the Father for the holy oil, with which he is going to anoint the sick person, he says: "By your Holy Spirit you have sanctified this oil in order that he may make us experience today the power of your love." In the *epiclese* or invocation for the blessing of the oil, the celebrant prays: "God, our Father, send your Holy Spirit, your Consoler, upon this oil that you have created, that it may become a safeguard of mind and body for everyone who is anointed with this ointment of heavenly healing, to relieve every pain, every weakness, every ailment of mind and body..."

The Holy Spirit, Principle of our Moral Life

The participation, that the Holy Spirit confers on us through the Sacrament, in the divine filiation of Christ, which makes of us adopted children of God, is not sufficient to make us live fully this filial life. In order to belong truly to his adoptive family, the child must acquire the manners or morals of his new parents, their language, their way of life, their thoughts and feelings. Likewise, having been introduced in the family of God as sons, we must strive to live as sons: we must be "imitators of God," as St. Paul says, "as very dear children" (Ep 5:1). We must strive to imitate our elder Brother, who is God's natural Son: Jesus Christ. We must think, love, act, feel and talk like him who is the natural son of the family, in whom the Father has adopted us as sons. We must become "conformed to the image of his Son, so that he may be the firstborn among many brothers" (Rm 8:29-30).

The transformation in question here, is not any longer the essential or ontological transformation, the radical transformation brought about by sanctifying grace received in Baptism. That consists in the casting away of the old man, vitiated by Original Sin, and in the putting on of the new man created in the image of God, in the initial act of our divinization through our communication with Jesus Christ, the Son of God; hence, by our adoption as children of God. It is a question here of another transformation: a transformation on the plane of conduct, a moral transformation.

St. Paul tells us of what this transformation consists. In his letter to the Ephesians, he writes: "You are to put off the old man, which is corrupted through its deceptive lusts. And be renewed in the spirit of your mind, and put on the new man, which has been created according to God in justice and holiness of truth" (Ep 4:23-24). And in Colossians, he says:

> *Mortify your members, which are on earth: immorality, uncleanness, lust, evil desire and covetousness . . . You once walked in them when they were your life. But now do you also put them away: anger, wrath, malice, abusive language and foul-mouthed utterances. Do not lie to one another. Strip off the old man with his deeds and put on the new, one that is being renewed unto perfect knowledge "according to the image of his Creator." . . .*

> *Put on therefore, as God's chosen ones, holy and beloved, a heart of mercy, kindness, humility, meekness, patience. Bear with one another and forgive one another, if anyone has a grievance against any other; even as the Lord has forgiven you, so also do you forgive. But above all have love, which is the bond of perfection. And may the peace of Christ reign in your hearts; unto that peace, indeed, you were called in one body. Show yourselves thankful. (Col 3:5-15).*

This moral transformation is the work of the Holy Spirit. The work of our conversion and our renewal according to the image of God in Christ surpasses absolutely the forces of our nature. It is a question of living as sons of God, of acquiring the morals of our heavenly Father, according to these words of St. Peter: "As obedient children, do not conform to the lusts of former days when you were ignorant; but as the One who called you is holy, be you also holy in all your behavior; for it is written, 'You shall be holy, because I am holy'" (1 P 1:14-16). Jesus himself had said: "You are to be perfect, even as your heavenly Father is perfect" (Mt 5:48). Our moral transformation, therefore, necessarily requires the dynamic intervention of the Power of God personified: the Holy Spirit: his permanent and unceasing intervention because this transformation is the work of a whole lifetime. The new man is continually renewed according to the image of his Creator" (Col 3:10), and that "the inner man is being renewed day by day" (2 Cor 4:16).

After he has transformed us on the plan of being, the Holy Spirit transforms us on the plane of conduct. He who has made us sons of God, also makes us act as sons of God, "since we live by the Spirit, by the Spirit let us live" (Gal 5:25). He makes us become what we are: sons of God. "If you live according to the flesh (to the old man), you die; but if by the Spirit you put to death the deeds of the flesh, you will live. For whoever are led by the Spirit of God, they are the sons of God" (Rm 8:13-14).

That is why, we offend in a special way the Holy Spirit with our evil conduct. "Do you not know that your members are the temple of the Holy Spirit, who is in you, whom you have from God" (1 Cor 6:19-20) "This is the will of God, your sanctification; that you abstain from immorality; that every one of you learn how to possess his vessel in holiness and honor, not in the passion of lust. . . ; that no one transgress and overreach his brother in the matter, because the Lord is the avenger of all these things, as we have told you before . . . For God has not called us unto uncleanness, but unto holiness. Therefore, he who rejects these things rejects not man but God, who has also given the Holy Spirit to us" (1 Th 4:3-8). Talking in a human way, the Apostle goes so far as to say that the Holy Spirit is affected by a conduct which is not in conformity with his transforming activity. "Do not grieve the Holy Spirit of God in whom you were sealed from the day of redemption. Let all bitterness, and wrath, and indignation, and clamor and reviling, be removed from you, along with all malice. On the contrary, be kind to one another, and merciful, generously forgiving one another, as also God in Christ has generously forgiven you" (Ep 4:30-32).

Among other reasons, because of the role played in our renewal on the plane of being and conduct the Holy Spirit is represented by the symbol of fire.

Insofar as he is the author of our divinization, as fire burns and consumes, the Holy Spirit makes the stain disappear radically; the stain which made us unpleasant in the sight of God. As fire is used in recasting a broken vase, so it is in the fire of the Holy Spirit, the fire of his love, that our being is baptized, plunged and recast, into a new being, a divinized being.

Also, the Holy Spirit is represented by the symbol of fire insofar as he is the principle of our moral transformation. As fire purifies gold, so the Holy Spirit works our purification: he burns, puts to death the old man and his evil deeds. As we test gold by fire to verify its authenticity, so the Holy Spirit plunges in the purifying crucible our faith, hope and love, precisely in order to purify them and make them more authentic—that he may unite us more intimately with God. St. John of the Cross compares the soul to a damp fire-log, which fire first starts by enveloping on the surface, and thus takes away its humidity and coldness. Similarly, the Holy Spirit begins our renewal by freeing our soul of its faults, pride, egoism and vices and having purified us, disposes by his "living flame of love" for the divine union, and the transformation of love in God.

Water too is an appropriate symbol for the Holy Spirit. As water washes and purifies, so the Holy Spirit brings about our purification. "I will put water in the desert," God said through his prophet Isaias, "and rivers in the wasteland for my chosen people to drink" (Is 43:20); "I will pour out water upon thirsty ground and streams upon the dry land. I will pour my Spirit upon your offspring" (44:3). Through Ezechiel, the Lord said: "I will sprinkle clean water upon you to cleanse you from all your impurities, and from all your idols I will cleanse you. I will give you a new heart and place a new Spirit within you" (Ezk 36:25-27). And our Lord called the Holy Spirit, "living water," and "water which springs up unto life everlasting."

It is above all by obedience to the commandments of God that the Holy Spirit works our moral transformation. The Holy Spirit is the very principle of the commandments. These are means whose end is to make us live and act as sons of God, to be "perfect as our heavenly Father is perfect." Now the means have to be adapted to the end. Our Lord has, therefore, perfected the commandments of the Old Law, so that by observing them, they could let us conduct ourselves according to our eminent condition of sons of God. "Do not think that I have come to destroy the Law and the Prophets. I have come not to destroy but to fulfill" (Mt 5:17). Indeed, Christ has not abolished the Law. A young man asked him: "Good Master, what good work shall I do to have eternal life?" Our Lord answered: "If thou wilt enter into life, keep the commandments." He said to him, 'Which?' And Jesus said, 'Thou shalt not kill, 'Thou shalt not commit adultery, Thou shalt not steal, Thou shalt not bear false witness, Honor thy father and mother, and Thou shalt love thy neighbor as thyself" (Mt 19:16-19). Another time, the Pharisee asked him, "Master, which is the great commandment in the Law?" Jesus said: "Thou shalt love the Lord thy God with thy whole heart and with thy whole soul, and with thy whole mind" (Mt 22:36-37). And then he added: "This is the greatest and the first commandment. And the second is like it, 'Thou shalt love thy neighbor as thyself.' "

Christ did not abolish the Law, he perfected it. Going over different commandments of the Law, he perfected them by stressing each corrective by the words: "You have heard that it was said to the ancients . . . But I say to you" (Mt 5:21-48). Thus the commandments given to Israel, recast and perfected, have become the commandments of Jesus. That is why, Jesus will say truthfully, "If you keep *my* commandments, you will abide in my love" (Jn 15:10). "If you love me, keep *my* commandments"; "He who has *my* commandments and keeps them, he it is who loves me" (Jn 14:15,21). It is so especially of the second commandment, "You shall love your neighbor as yourself," which he made his commandment, perfecting it into a *new* commandment: "A *new* commandment I give you, that you love one another; that as I have loved you, you also love one another" (Jn 13:34); "This is *my* commandment, that you love one another *as I have loved you*" (Jn 15:12).

Jesus perfected the commandments not only by clearing them of all that men had added to them, but also by interiorizing them. He did so by giving us the possibility to observe them, not in an exterior and formalist manner, or because of the fear of punishment, but from love. In fact, after having given to the Pharisee the answer, cited above, Jesus added: "On these two commandments depend the whole law and the Prophets" (Mt 22:40). St. Paul commented on the Lord's words thus: "He who loves his neighbor has fulfilled the Law. For, 'Thou shalt not commit adultery; Thou shalt not kill; Thou shalt not steal; Thou shalt not covet;' and if there is any other commandment, it is summed up in this saying, 'Thou shalt love thy neighbor as thyself.' Love does no evil to a neighbor. Love therefore is the fulfillment of the Law" (Rm 13:8-10).

Christ interiorized the commandments by attaching them to love as to their unique principle; and has transformed them into instruments of freedom. Thanks to Christ the Law, of which the commandments are the expression, has become the new Law. The new Law promised by God in the Old Testament says: " 'This is the covenant which I will make with the house of Israel after those days', says the Lord. 'I will place my law within them, and write it upon their hearts' " (Jr 31:33). He has actually written this law in the hearts of Christians. This has been accomplished by his Spirit of Love, as St Paul explains to the Corinthians: "You are a letter of Christ composed by us, written not with ink but in the Spirit of the living God, not on tablets of stone but on fleshly tablets of the heart" (2 Cor 3:3). This law is sanctifying grace, the dynamic power of the "faith working through love" (Gal 5:6). It is "the love of God poured forth in our hearts by the Holy Spirit who has been given to us" (Rm 5:5). The new law is the Holy Spirit himself, the Spirit of Love.

The new law must be a law of freedom, for love is essentially free. The word liberty recurs constantly under the pen of the Apostle to describe the new law, or the presence of the Holy Spirit in us: "the liberty which we have in Christ Jesus" (Gal 2:4); "where the Spirit of the Lord is, there is freedom" (2 Cor 3:18). St. James says: "who has carefully looked into the perfect law of liberty and has remained in it, not becoming a forgetful hearer but a doer of the words, shall be blessed in his deeds" (Jm 1:25); "So speak and act as men about to be judged by the law of liberty" (2:12).

The commandments which express exteriorly the new law, the law of liberty, can be only instruments of freedom and the obedience to them begets liberation itself, from the slavery of fear. Interiorized, the commandments free us from the fear of punishment, since the new law asks that we obey them from love. "The children of God," writes St. Thomas, "are led by the Holy Spirit, freely, under the impulse of love and not at all as slaves by fear ... A slave refrains only from the fear of the law, the evil which he continues to desire" (*Contra Gent.*). Moreover, "there is no fear in love," says St. John, "but perfect love casts out fear, because fear brings punishment. And he who fears is not perfected in love" (1 Jn 4:18).

Also there is liberation from the slavery of Original Sin, namely, of the old man, of our proud and egotistical self, as well of our evil tendencies, which enslave our freedom. The commandments have for an end to free us little by little, by submitting us more and more to love, the soul of the commandments. Thanks to them, there takes place the spiritual liberation of our freedom by love, by the Holy Spirit, who is Love.

How far are we from the conception that many moderns have of the commandments, who make their cry of revolt and mockery of Andre Gode:

> *Commandments of God, you have made my soul ache.*
> *Commandments of God, are you ten or twenty?*
> *How far will you narrow your limits?*
> *Will you teach that there are always more things forbidden?*
> *New punishments assured to the thirst of all*
> *that I may have founf beautiful on earth?*
> *Commandments of God, you have made my soul ill.*
> *You have surrounded by walls the only waters*
> *to quench my thirst.* (Gide. *Les nourritures terrestres*)

Envisaged as a law of love, far from being pure prohibitions that vex us, far from being prescriptions imposed on us under the tiresome and withering form of repression, these commandments appear to us as means that aim at nothing else than to expand us, to obtain the liberation of our souls, not by the mutilation of our nature but by the rectification of its disordered tendencies, by the mortification of the *ego* which shuts the entrance of our heart, and by its opening to love.

By becoming the interior principle of the commandments, the

Holy Spirit or Love, frees us, in a certain way, from the commandments themselves. It is thus that the Holy Spirit proves itself to be also the principle of obedience. What matters basically is not the obedience to the commandments for themselves, but love which animates this obedience. Because the Holy Spirit is the new law, because he vivifies us interiorly with his love, it is by love that we are inclined to do good and avoid evil, without having to have the commandments prescribe one and prohibit the other. "The fruit of the Spirit (i.e., of the man regenerated by grace and vivified by the Holy Spirit) is love, joy, peace, patience, kindness, goodness, trust, modesty, continency. Against those who live this way there is no law" (Gal 5:22-23). St. Paul writes to Timothy: "the Law is not made for the just" (1 Tm 1:9). The just man is he who practices the commandments of love. St. Paul tells us that love is "the fulfillment of the Law."

This is what St. Paul calls "the freedom of the children of God" (Rm 8:21), and what made St. Augustine say: "*Diliges, et quod vis fac*; Love and do what you want." We must understand these famous words of St. Augustine, words that some invoke in order to permit themselves the worst moral excesses. These words must be understood in the light of what St. Paul said, quoted above, "Love does no evil to the neighbor." Love, then does not dispense us from obeying the other commandments; and our neighbor must be able to say to us: "If you really love me, you will not dishonor conjugal fidelity; you will not kill me; you will not hit me; you will not steal my goods; you will not testify falsely against me; you will not envy me; you will not covet my goods, and so forth. Really love me and you will be free to do what you want, for then your love for me will prevent you from hurting me since love does no evil to the neighbor."

By placing love as the principle of moral life, we do not abolish the moral law, i.e., abolish the commandments for the benefit of one only. Love does not suppress the commandments. Indeed, because it is difficult for us, not to say well-nigh impossible, to become, here on earth, a truly interior and spiritual person, entirely docile to the interior law, totally possessed by the Holy Spirit; because we remain liable to sinning on account of our inclination to evil, of the triple concupiscence of which St. John speaks, we need to be guided by a direction, exterior to us so that we may not be deceived in the choice of means that may lead us to God. It is in this that lies the role of the commandments of the Lord.

The commandments continue to exist in order to serve us as guide marks for the options of our freedom. In other words we are free of them; we are free from their letter, which kills when it is not vivified by the Spirit, by love. This is the primary role given to love to assure our liberation in respect to the commandments. Without love we are their slaves. With love we accept the commandments to go to God freely but surely. "He who avoids evil," says St. Thomas, "not because it is evil, but because of a commandment of the Lord, is not free. He is free who avoids evil because it is evil. Now, it is that which the Holy Spirit accomplishes; he perfects interiorly the soul by communicating to it a new dynamic force, in such a way that it has by love the same care to avoid evil, if the divine law demanded it. That is why we call it free, not that it is not subject to the law, but because its interior dynamic love makes it do what the divine law commands." Obedience to our Lord does not have value unless it is inspired by love, and unless it expresses love.

In these conditions obedience becomes docility to the Spirit of Christ and constitutes the true liberty of the children of God. This liberty, far from destroying human freedom, realizes it since this liberty for the will consists in self-determination. For freedom is not, as it is currently believed, the power to do the good or the evil indifferently. It is the power of the will to choose the good, and to do so spontaneously, without being impelled to it by anything but the good itself. Now, it is the Spirit of Christ who inclines the will, through the weight of love, to go spontaneously toward the good. Thanks to the intervention of the Holy Spirit, in our obedience to the commandments, we practice an obedience befitting sons of God, an obedience of love.

The Holy Spirit does not only vivify us and make us act supernaturally. He leads us and moves us. "Those are sons of God," says St. Paul, "who are led by the Spirit of God" (Rm 8:14). And in Galatians, he says, "Let yourself be conducted by the Spirit, and you will not fulfill the lusts of the flesh" (Gal 5:16). To make us fit to be acted upon and to be led by him, the Holy Spirit confers on us certain gifts. These gifts are energies and dispositions making more effective the actions of the theological and moral virtues; and more prompt, more eager our response to the inspirations of the Holy Spirit.

These gifts are many. The Church has identified some: the six which are listed in Isaiah 11:2, to which she has added a seventh. Here they are: the gift of fear, of piety, of knowledge, of fortitude, of counsel, of understanding and that of wisdom.

Wisdom helps us to find delight in the contemplation of divine things, also by divine principles to judge of things human as well as divine; *understanding* helps us to grasp the credibility of the mysteries of faith; *counsel* puts us on our guard against the deceits of the devil and the world, and helps us in dubious cases to see what is more to the glory of God and more conducive to our own and our neighbor's salvation; *fortitude* affords us remarkable strength in resisting temptation and overcoming hindrances to our spiritual life; *knowledge* helps us to distinguish rightly between what we should do and should not believe; by it, too, we are guided in those things which concern our spiritual life; *piety* shows how to offer due worship to God; it shows us how, for the love of God, to assist those who are in trouble; *fear of the Lord* helps us to avoid offending our Father in heaven; this fear springs from a reverential and filial love of God.

These gifts of the Holy Spirit are *permanent* qualities; they remain in us, but they can slumber, become sluggish. We have to bring out their value by exercising them. We must open our hearts unceasingly to the "inspirations" of the Spirit of love, who breathes where he wills and when he wills.

Thus, through the work of our freedom and of the Holy Spirit, who acts in us in the Sacraments and in our obedience to the commandments of the Lord, we are progressively transformed, according to the image of Jesus Christ the same Spirit, as St. Paul told the Corinthians: "We all, with faces unveiled reflecting as in a mirror the glory of the Lord, are being transformed into his very image from glory to glory, as through the Spirit of our Lord" (2 Cor 3:18).

CHAPTER NINE

The Holy Spirit in the Church

We have seen how the promise of the Father and the Son to send the Holy Spirit in the world was realized with the descent of the Holy Spirit upon the disciples gathered at the Cenacle the day of Pentecost when the Church whose foundations had already been laid was definitely established. In this chapter, we shall see that the Holy Spirit presided at her establishment and made of the Church one, holy, catholic and apostolic, because he is the principle of her unity and consequently of her catholicity, holiness and apostolicity. He is also the principle who acts through her unifying organs of government and in the means of her unification.

"Christ, the one Mediator," says Vatican II, "established and ceaselessly sustains here on earth His holy Church, the community of faith, hope and charity, as a visible structure. Through her he communicates truth and grace to all. But the society furnished with hierarchical agencies and the Mystical Body of Christ are not to be considered as two realities, nor are the visible assembly and the spiritual community, nor the earthly Church and the Church enriched with heavenly things. Rather they form one interlocked reality which is comprised of a divine and a human element" (Const. *Lumen Gentium*, #8).

The Council has recalled thus that the Church of Christ has two aspects: a visible aspect and an invisible aspect. She is a society organized hierarchically (an institution), and she is also a spiritual community (a communion of faith, hope and love). Both institution and communion form a unique reality, which the Council calls by the biblical name of *people of God*. The conciliar Constitution, in order to characterize the Church adequately, had already used images taken from Scripture and "drawn from pastoral life, agriculture, building construction, and even from family and married life," images which "served a preparatory role in the writings of the prophets" (#6). The Church is a sheepfold, a flock, the field of God, the vineyard of God, the temple of God, the house of God, the kingdom of God, the bride of Christ, the Body of Christ. However, it is the term *people of God* which prevailed because of its universal significance, and from the fact that the Church journeys toward the Lord through human history. It is a most apt term also because it stresses the essential tie of the Church with the ancient people of God, with the children of Abraham.

The Holy Spirit, Soul of the Church as a Spiritual Community

The conciliar Fathers have avoided presenting the Church, from the very beginning of *Lumen Gentium*, as a juridical society and a hierarchical institution, what she is also actually but which does not express her essential mystery, which is a mystery of communion. Indeed, the Church is not primarily a vast organization, structured more or less efficiently and ruled by a code of laws, composed principally by a hierarchy and a body of professional cadres, to whom some hundreds of millions of people more or less obey. The Church is, first and foremost, a human-divine community which calls the whole of humanity to a most profound unity, safeguarding the personality of each man, because her mission is to unite them to God, by gathering all in the faith of Christ—in the same living organism, the Body of Christ, through the Holy Spirit, for time and eternity.

The unity of love which was planned by God for mankind and which constituted the original order of humanity, was compromised by the sin of Adam, the first sin of man, and even destroyed by the effects of sin. And when men had become sufficiently numerous and wanted to establish the unity of the world by themselves and without reference to God, they constructed the Tower of Babel, as a gathering place of the humanity of that time. Their attempt failed and ended up in the division and the scattering of the peoples, and the confusion of tongues.

Jesus Christ, the New Adam, has come in the world to

reestablish this unity. "God," says St. Paul, "has made known to us the mystery of his will . . . in the fullness of the times: to reestablish all things in Christ" (Ep 1:9-10). And St. John writes: "Jesus was to die ... that he might gather into one the children of God who were scattered abroad" (Jn 11:52).

This unity, for which Christ died, is not any ordinary union, it is not a unity of juxtaposition, order or cooperation, similar to a political society, but a unity of being, of life and of love: a unity like the unity existing among the Persons of the Holy Trinity. "That they all may be one," our Lord asked of the Father, "even as thou, Father, in me and I in thee; that they also may be one in us . . . that they be perfected in unity" (Jn 17:21-23).

To elucidate the mystery of the intimate character of this unity among Christians, St. Paul compares the union to an organic, vital organism, which exists in the members of the human body. "We, though many, are one body in Christ," he wrote to the Romans (Rm 12:5); and to the Corinthians: "For as the body is one and has many members, and all the members of the body, many as they are, form one body, so it is with Christ. For in one Spirit we were all baptized into one body" (1 Cor 12:12-13). Like the bodily members are united in one living organism, thanks to the unity of life which animates them, the life of Christ, which he communicates to Christians, they are also united in an essential, profound and vital union. This comparison with the human body must be understood not only as an image or as an unattainable ideal to imitate, but as a *reality*.

In taking a human body, Christ established the new order, destined to realize unity among men; reestablished, the original order, the order of love—similar to the Trinitarian unity. By uniting men to his Body, Christ its Head, unites them as the members of a human body are united by their union to this one body. Consequently, the Church is to be identified as the Body of Christ. That is what St. Paul did. "Do you not know," he wrote to the Corinthians, "that your bodies are members of Christ?" (1 Cor 6:16). Later, he tells them: "You are the body of Christ, member for member" (1 Cor 12:27). In Ephesians, he speaks of "the Church, which indeed is Christ's body" (Ep 1:22-23); and to the Collosians he says: "Christ is the head of his body, the Church" (Col 1:18); and "I rejoice now in the sufferings I bear for your sake; and what is lacking of the sufferings of Christ I fill up in my flesh for his body, which is the Church" (1:24).

The Semitic notion of the body, which was that of St. Paul, does not correspond exactly to our notion. Semites do not separate the body from the principle which animates it. The body designates the whole of man, in his concrete reality of a living person—with the stress on its visible, sensible aspect. Thus St. Paul replaces, several times, the word body by a personal pronoun as in this passage: "Even thus ought husbands also to love their wives as their own bodies. He who loves his own wife, loves himself" (Ep 5:28). To belong to the body of Christ is equivalent to belonging to Christ himself, the *corporeal* Christ. Inversely, to be in Christ is equivalent to being in his body. And "the Church is the Body of Christ" signifies that she is Christ himself, but existing corporeally.

It goes without saying that the body of Christ of which we are speaking is his glorious body, hence spiritual. The unity of the faithful with him is of the spiritual order. That is why St. Paul could say: "He who cleaves to the Lord is one spirit with him" (1 Cor 6:17).

The principle of unity of this body of Christ which has been called since the Middle Ages, the Mystical Body, in order to distinguish it from the Eucharistic Body, is the Holy Spirit. Since the Church is the body of Christ, isn't the Holy Spirit the principle of this spiritual unity? Didn't St. John say that "Jesus was to die in order that he might gather in one the children of God who were scattered abroad? However, Christ and his Spirit have each a role to play in this work of unification.

Christ has merited and gained the unity of mankind through his death and Resurrection. The redemptive work of Christ has for its end the union of men with God, by reconciliating them with him. "God," writes St. Paul, "has reconciled us to himself through Christ ... For God was truly in Christ, reconciling the world to himself" (2 Cor 5:17-19). Christ reconciled us to God "through the blood of his cross" (Col 1:20). But Christ's redemptive work also aims at uniting men among themselves. Again it is St. Paul who speaks lyrically about the divine event:

> *Bear in mind that once you, the Gentiles in flesh, . . . were at that time without Christ, excluded as aliens from the*

community of Israel, and strangers to the covenants of the promise; having no hope, and without God in the world. But now in Christ Jesus you, who were once afar off, have been brought near through the blood of Christ. For he himself is our peace, *he it is who* has made both one, *and has broken down the intervening wall of the enclosure, the enmity, in his flesh. The Law of the commandments expressed in decrees he has made void, that of the two (peoples) he might create in himself one new man, and make peace, and reconcile both in* one body *to God by the cross, having slain the enmity in himself. And coming, he announced the good tidings of peace to you who were afar off . . . and to those who were near; because through him we both have access in one Spirit to the Father . . . You are now built upon the foundation of the apostles and prophets with Christ Jesus himself as the chief cornerstone. In him the whole structure is closely fitted together into a temple holy in the Lord; in him you too are being built together into a dwelling place for God in the Spirit* (Ep 2:11-22).

Christ has not only gained the union with the Church through his blood, he is also the foundation of the Church. The union realized by Christ's death is a union of being, life and love. Now, only the Church can obtain this kind of union for mankind, for only she has for her constitutive principle, or for essential foundation of her unity, a *living person*: the Son of God become Man, Jesus Christ. In the order of nature, there does not, nor can there be, a concrete universal person, who assembles and summarizes (in himself) all human persons. A biological dependence of this sort on a super-being cannot be conceived. The state itself, however totalitarian, is not a superman. Only the Church can achieve such unity for the members because the living person who is the constitutive principle of this unity is a divine Person. By dying and rising up again, our Lord, though remaining what he was, Son of man as well as Son of God, became "a living spirit," the mystical, *pneumatic* or the spiritual Christ. And as such he unites mankind in himself, in a union not only of the intellectual and psychological order, but also of the ontological order. This is a union by identification of Christ with the Christians.

Christians are, according to the favorite term of St. Paul, "in Christ," as I discussed in another chapter, drawing from the works of Emile Mersch. Christians exist *in Christ*. The glorious Christ can be considered as an "existential milieu," where the whole being of man is taken up by a new principle, and is created *anew*. Men enter this milieu to be transformed in "a unique man, a unique body," one new man, who is the corporeal Christ. Christ and Christians form then one and the same being, though they are many persons. The union of the members of the Church is founded on Christ. They communicate one with another because they are all "in Christ." "There is neither Jew nor Greek; there is neither slave nor freeman; there is neither male nor female. For you are all one in Christ Jesus" (Gal 3:28); "Here there is not 'Gentile and Jew,' 'circumcised and uncircumcised,' 'Barbarian and Scythian,' 'slave and freeman;' but Christ is all things and in all" (Col 3:10-11). "So we, though many, are one body in Christ, and individually members one of another" (Rm 12:5).

The identification of Christ and the Christians is not only a community of being, but also a community of life.

Because they are "in Christ," Christians live the life of Christ. St. Paul expresses this supernatural reality in burning words: "It is now no longer I that live, but Christ lives in me. And this life that I now live in the flesh, I live in the faith of the Son of God, who loved me and gave himself up for me" (Gal 2:20-21). This life is the very life of God. In his Person of the Word Incarnate, Christ communicates to Christians his divine nature that he enables men to find again their lost unity. "The glory (divine nature, divine love) that thou hast given me, I have given to them," Jesus prayed to his Father at the Last Supper, "that they may become one, even as we are one; I in them and thou in me, that they may be perfected in unity" (Jn 17:22-23). The unity of Christians is founded in God himself who is in Christ, living in each of them. "One God and Father of all," writes St. Paul, "who is above all, and throughout all, and in us all" (Ep 4:5-6). That's why, in heaven, the unity will perfect, for then "God will be all in all" (1 Cor 15:28). By this supernatural life, flowing from God through Christ, Christians are blood relations. They form one family of children of God; they are brothers, and Christ is "the firstborn among many brethren" (Rm 8:29).

Jesus Christ pervades the Church as the ontological and vital foundation upon which she is built. The power that established the Church upon this foundation, through the communication to her of the being and life of Christ, is the Holy Spirit. According to St. Paul: "In Christ Jesus you are built together into a dwelling place for God in the Spirit" (Ep 5:21); and "For as the body is one and has many members, and all the members of the body, many as they are, form one body, so also is it with Christ. For in one Spirit we were all baptized into one body, whether Jews or Gentiles, whether slaves or free; and we were all given to drink of one Spirit" (1 Cor 12:12-13).

The inner unity of the Church can only be the work of the Holy Spirit, like the unity which exists between the three divine Persons. The Holy Spirit who unites in him the Father and the Son, also unites the members of the Mystical Body among themselves, and at the same time unites them to him who is their head, Christ Jesus. It is the Spirit who communicates to the members of the Church the being and the life of Christ. The simultaneous presence of the Holy Spirit in Christ and in the faithful assures the ontological and vital union between the head and the members of the Mystical Body, and hence among the members themselves.

According to St. Thomas, the most profound union is the one which is brought about in something which is numerically one. Now the Holy Spirit is numerically one and the same in the head and in the members of the Mystical Body. He is thus able to unite the members of the Church in the most profound unity possible. "It is to the Spirit of Christ as the one indivisible principle," wrote Pius XII, "that we must attribute the fact that all the parts of the Body are united, among themselves as well as with their Head, since the Spirit dwells wholly in the Head, wholly in the Body, wholly into each member" (Encycl. *Mistici Corporis Christi*). It is the unicity of the Holy Spirit which brings about the marvellous unity of the Church. Pope Leo XII rightly wrote that "if Christ is the head of the Church, the Holy Spirit is her soul" (Encycl. *Divinum illud munus*).

The Holy Spirit is then to the Mystical Body what the soul is to the human body: the principle of the unity of the members, the principle which makes this unity. And it should be so, since the Holy Spirit is Love personified. And love creates the most perfect union, as St. Paul wrote to the Collosians: "Above all have love which is the most perfect bond (the bond of perfection)" (Col 3:14). The same

Apostle also said the following, which I have quoted already several times: "The love of God is poured forth in our hearts by the Holy Spirit who has been given to us" (Rm 5:5). It is the Holy Spirit who vivifies the members of Christ and effects their unity. They should become aware of this through a vivid faith, participate in this unity by love, communicate in this mystery of unity so that they may communicate in the mystery of the Father and the Son, united by their common Spirit of Love: "That they all be one as we are one!"

Soul of the Church, the Holy Spirit is also the principle of her spread throughout the world. Taking possession of the Apostles at Pentecost, the Holy Spirit communicated to the newly-born Church his dynamic energy. No sooner had he descended upon them than the Apostles began to proclaim the wonders of God and to announce the good news of salvation. From that day on, an era began, which we can call the era of the Holy Spirit. Obeying their Lord, the Apostles set out to proclaim the Gospel to every creature. Wherever they went they found churches. St. Luke wrote about those churches of Judea, Galilee and Samaria: "The Church was being built up, walking in fear of the Lord, and it was filled with the aid and joy of the Holy Spirit" (Ac 9:31).

St. Luke shows the Holy Spirit at work in this first expansion of the Church among pagans. He tells the episode of the evangelization and the conversion by St. Peter of the Roman centurion Cornelius and his household. "When Peter was still speaking these words (about Jesus Christ), the Holy Spirit came upon all who were listening to his message. And the faithful of the circumcision, who had come with Peter were amazed because on the Gentiles also the grace of the Holy Spirit had been poured forth; for they heard them speaking in tongues and magnifying God. Then Peter answered, 'Can anyone refuse the water to baptize these, seeing that they have received the Holy Spirit just as we did?' And he ordered them to be baptized in the name of Jesus Christ" (Ac 10:44-48; 15:7-8).

Like the primitive Church, it is under the breath of the Holy Spirit that the Church continues to spread in the world. The expansion of the Church is not an accidental activity, but it is part of her very essence. The Church is Catholic by her nature, for she is essentially universal, and she is the community which calls to unity people of all times and all countries. She was set up for the whole of humanity, and until she has gathered together in her unity all humanity, she will seek to expand. Thus she is essentially missionary. Her expansion through the centuries is the manifestation of her internal vitality, her capacity and power to gather all mankind in Christ. The Church carries a message which concerns all human beings, a message which responds fully to the most profound aspirations of their being—which consequently exists in everyone. Even though many pervert or suppress this message the yearning for a total love, which is no other than a yearning for God, who is Love persists.

The Church is universal because her nature is love, as is the nature of her founder. Now divine love is poured in the Church by the Holy Spirit, who has been given to her. Through the Church, the Holy Spirit spreads love through the World. That is why for Eastern theology, the Church is the mystery of the outpouring of the Spirit in the history of salvation, and the time of the Church in this history is called the "Economy of the Spirit."

This universalist note of the Church explains her exterior unity and her holiness, and it presupposes with them her apostolicity. There too the Holy Spirit plays a primordial role.

Because the Church is the community which calls for the universal unity of mankind, she has to be one, unique. "There is one Body and one Spirit," says St. Paul. In fact, there is only one Church because there is only one body of Christ and one Spirit. For "a second visible Body of Christ, a second visible manifestation of his Spirit," says Karl Adam, "are as inconceivable as a second Christ."

Being the one Body of Christ, animated by a unique Spirit and having for her mission the unity of all mankind, the Church is holy. She is holy not in the sense that she does not contain in her fold sinners, but because she is the Body of Christ, who is holy and who has loved her as his Bride and had delivered himself to sanctify her, and has made her members partake of his divine holiness. Now it is the Holy Spirit who brings about this participation by communicating to them sanctifying grace, thus making them holy. He is the Spirit of holiness. "Christians," says St. Peter, "are chosen unto the sanctification of the Spirit, according to the plan of God, unto obedience to Jesus Christ" (1 P 1:2).

Finally, the internal and external unity of the Church, as well as her catholicity and holiness presuppose necessarily her apostolicity, namely, her original and actual foundation on the twelve Apostles. St. Paul says that the Church "has for foundation the Apostles and the Prophets" (Ep 2:20). Christ said to St. Peter: "Thou art Peter and upon this rock I will build my Church" (Mt 16:18). Moreover, history tells us that she has always been united with the Apostles by a continuity of Popes and bishops. Of this apostolicity also the Spirit is the principle. We know that Jesus acted always under the inspiration of the Holy Spirit. Under the inspiration of the Spirit that the Lord chose the Apostles, and it is the Holy Spirit who has kept and will continue to keep the tie of the Church with the college of the Apostles, thus assuring their successors an uninterrupted apostolic continuity.

The Holy Spirit in the Church as an Hierarchical Society

The Holy Spirit is not only the principle which constitutes the unity of the Church, and which makes her grow in numbers and in holiness in one body. His action also exerts itself in those who preside over this unification and growth as well as in the means applied for these ends.

To bring about the unity of the Church and her expansion, Christ has appointed the Apostles and their successors, the bishops, who form what we call the hierarchy. These prolong his mission by serving the people of God.

The Catholic hierarchy is much more than a mere function of authority, a directive organ indispensable to every human society for order and discipline, and to lead it to its end. It is really the extension of the action of Christ, who came in the world "not to be served, but to serve." It is by the visible members of the hierarchy that the invisible action of Christ reaches mankind, even if these members have faults, as other men do, provided that they exercise their functions in their particular competence and that they do not ordain what would constitute a sin; also provided that they act within conditions set by the will of Christ. It is this tie with Christ which gives the *raison d'etre* or the reason for its existence to the Catholic hierarchy.

In extending in a visible manner the salvific work of the Son of

God, the hierarchy prolongs the work of God the Father, who, according to St. Paul, "was in Christ reconciling the world to himself." Moreover, "he who sees me," our Lord said, "sees also the Father." Being, in a way, the visible continuation of Christ, the hierarchy makes present and prolongs the manifestation, in Christ, of the Fatherhood of God towards men. A bishop is for his particular church, the image of the Father. At the beginning of the 2nd century, St. Ignatius of Antioch, could write to the Christians of Magnesia: "It is the very power of God the Father that you must revere in your bishop. It is not to him, your bishop, that your submission goes, but to the Father of Jesus Christ, to the universal bishop" (*Letter to the Magnesians*). It is for this reason that the bishop of the universal Church, the Bishop of Rome, is called the "Pope," or the "Holy Father." But the name "Father" is not reserved to him alone; it belongs, by the same right, to every bishop of a particular church, for each, before being the pastor of his own particular flock, is the shepherd of the whole Church, with the Pope and with the other bishops—under the authority of the Pope, the supreme Pastor and the center of Catholic unity.

As the incarnation of the Fatherhood of God, the hierarchy must, like the Father, give the Son to the world. Now, the work of Christ, or of the Father, which the hierarchy prolongs, is accomplished by the Holy Spirit, under the dynamic thrust of love, like the Father and the Son. "God so loved the world that he gave his only-begotten Son," as Jesus said. It is then through the Holy Spirit that the hierarchy exercises its work and power.

Actually the authority of the hierarchy originates from the Holy Spirit. It is he who appoints its trustees by giving them the charism attached to this ministry. St. Paul advises the presbyters of the Church of Ephesus thus: "Take heed to yourselves and to the whole flock in which the Holy Spirit has placed you as bishops to rule the Church of God" (Ac 20:28). It is also the Holy Spirit who directs the hierarchy in its decision so much so that these are really his decisions, as the ancients at the first Council of Jerusalem declared: "For the Holy Spirit and we ourselves have decided" (Ac 15:28). Every action that injures or undermines the authority of the hierarchy, affects the Holy Spirit in person. Thus St. Peter reproaches Ananias and Sapphira as having deceived the Holy Spirit himself in deceiving the

Apostles, when by fraud they kept back part of the price of the land that they were to give to the Christian community at Jerusalem (cf. Ac 5:1-11).

Since things are that way, it is erroneous to oppose the two aspects of the Church, namely, the Church-institution and the Church-people-of-God: the visible Church which rules, and the prophetic and spiritual Church. Many of our contemporaries are subject to the temptation of opposing, as an irreconcilable thesis and anti-thesis, the interior kingdom and the visible kingdom, the profound reality which constitutes the Mystical Body and the subordinate but necessary reality of the Institution, the "religion of the Spirit," and the "religion of authority." This temptation is not new; it has come up practically in every generation since the birth of the Church.

The kingdom which the Son of God has come to establish on earth, which was inaugurated at Pentecost, and which will find its glorious flowering at the end of time, is an interior spiritual kingdom, hidden in each individual soul. Every Christian in the state of grace has the privilege to be the temple of the Holy Spirit, to be "moved by the Spirit," and there is no intermediary between him and the Spirit. However, it is no less certain that the Spirit cannot be received— normally at least, or *de jure*—but in the Church and through the Church. And they who have received him are moved to remain united to the Church. The Church is a necessary means, the place *(milieu)* of the Spirit. St. Irenaeus said: "Where the Church is, there is also the Spirit of God; and where the Spirit of God is, there also is the Church and the plenitude of grace."

Human nature is not a pure spiritual or angelic nature; it is ill and corrupted by many defects, not to mention diabolical deceptive suggestions. The result is that spiritual things are perceived by the conscience only with many uncertainties, and through all sorts of distortions, which modern psychology of the unconscious or subconscious has shown with a new penetration. It is extremely difficult to discern the authentic interior inspirations of the Holy Spirit from the illusions and fantasies of our imagination. For every genuine mystic, how many misguided and deluded ones! It is necessary that a competent authority protect religious people from the deviations of their fantasy, or from the deceits of the evil one; and to verify by its guarantee the true message of the Spirit.

Who is moved by the Holy Spirit is, by that very fact, moved to integrate himself in the Church, in the hierarchical place that belongs to him in this grand supernatural organism. One cannot possess the Spirit of Christ without belonging—at least by the rectitude of his intention—to his Body which is the Church.

We should remain faithful to the hierarchy of the Church so that we may follow to the end the interior call of the Spirit. There will be difficult and painful moments when it would seem to us that we have to choose between obedience to the Spirit and obedience to the visible Church. There have been numerous tragic examples of this confrontation or choice in all ages of history, with the most disastrous results. How many people have separated themselves from the Church under the pretext of having to obey the Spirit! On the other hand, how many have been rewarded with a fruitful existence in the Church because in the hour of trial they have humbly let the Church decide whether they were obeying the Spirit or not!

Finally, the Holy Spirit plays a capital role in the means that Christ has given to his Church to gather in unity the children of God who are scattered in the world. The mission confided to the Church consists in leading men to believe in Christ by the proclamation of the Gospel, to communicate the life of Christ through the administration of the Sacraments, and to form in them Christ by the pastoral ministry. To attain this end, Christ has supplied the hierarchy with three powers: to preach the word of God to men, to administer to them the Sacraments and to give them pastoral direction in their observance of his commandments. "All power in heaven and on earth has been given to me. Go, therefore, and make disciples of all nations, baptizing them in the name of the Father, and of the Son, and of the Holy Spirit, teaching them to observe all that I have commanded you" (Mt 28:18-20). The Holy Spirit intervenes in the exercise of each of these means.

The first means lies in the power of the Church to speak in the place of God, to be the mouth by which God speaks to men: the power to proclaim the Word of God, in order to lead men to the faith, to believe the good news of salvation brought to us by Jesus Christ. For, "how are people to believe him (the Lord)," asks St. Paul, "whom they have not heard? And how are they to hear, if no one preaches?" And he concludes: "Faith, then, comes through hearing, and what is heard is the word of Christ" (Rm 10:14-17).

The word of God has been fully revealed in Jesus Christ and by Jesus Christ, who is the Word of God himself become man. In Jesus Christ and by Jesus Christ, God has spoken to men, as much as he could do it, in the historical conditions in which mankind finds itself at the present. Now, when God continues to speak to me in the Church and through the Church, it is in Jesus Christ and by Jesus Christ, living and acting in her, that God does so. That's why, the message of the preacher, provided he is faithful to the word of God contained in Scripture, though human in its form and words, is divine in its content. "We give thanks to God," St. Paul tells the Thessalonians, "because when you heard and received from us the word of God, you welcomed it not as the word of men, but as it truly is, the word of God" (1 Th 2:13).

The Holy Spirit ensures the perfect exercise of this power of the Church to announce the Word of God. The Acts of the Apostles manifests in numerous places this intervention of the Holy Spirit. It is he who chooses the apostle and sends him to proclaim the good news. "As they were ministering to the Lord and fasting, the Holy Spirit said, 'Set apart for me Saul and Barnabas unto the work to which I have called them.' Then, having fasted and prayed and laid their hands upon them, they let them go. So they, sent forth by the Holy Spirit, went to Seleucia and from there sailed to Cyprus" (Ac 13:2-5). It is the Holy Spirit who inspires the deacon Philip to approach the "minister of Candace, queen of Ethiopia, who had come to Jerusalem to worship and was returning in his carriage," and to announce to him the "good news of Jesus" (Ac 8:26-40). The Holy Spirit guides the preachers in their apostolic journeys. Thus he traces the itinerary of Paul and Silas: "Paul and Silas," narrates St. Luke, "passed through Phrygia and the Galatian country, for they were forbidden by the Holy Spirit to speak the word in the province of Asia. And when they came to Mysia, they tried to get into Bithynia, but the Spirit of Jesus did not permit them; so passing by Mysia, they went down to Troas" (Ac 16:6-7).

Moreover, the Apostles announce Jesus Christ because they are animated by the mighty breath of the Spirit of love. That is what St. Luke expresses with a phrase that he uses numerous times: "Filled with the Holy Spirit" (Ac 4:8; 6:3; 13:9), or "Full of the Spirit and of faith" (Ac 6:5; 11:24). This overflowing presence of the Holy Spirit inspires in the preachers their words and confers to them a force of persuasion which carries along the conviction and the adhesion of their listeners. Thus St. Paul can say to the Corinthians: "My speech and my preaching were not in the persuasive words of wisdom, but in the demonstration of the Spirit and of power, that your faith might rest, not on the wisdom of men, but on the power of God" (1 Cor 2:4-5). And to the Romans: "I do not make bold to mention anything but what Christ has wrought through me to bring about the obedience of the Gentiles, by word and deed, with mighty signs and wonders, by the power of the Holy Spirit" (Rm 15:18-19). This power of persuasion is pointed out by St. Luke when he tells about the dispute of St. Stephen with the Jews at Jerusalem. "Now Stephen, full of grace and power, was working great wonders and signs among the people. But there arose some from the synagogue which is called that of the Freedmen . . . disputing with Stephen. And they were not able to withstand the wisdom and the Spirit who spoke" (Ac 6:8-10). Jesus had foretold to his disciples this special intervention of the Holy Spirit, especially when they would be persecuted. "But when they deliver you up, do not be anxious how or what you are to speak; for what you are to speak will be given you in that hour. For it is not you who are speaking, but the Spirit of your Father who speaks through you" (Mt 10:19-20).

To verify their preaching, the Apostles gave witness to Jesus Christ. They were able to do that through the power of the Holy Spirit, as their Lord had foretold them. Thus St. Peter answered the High Priest, who "charged him not to preach in Jesus' name:" "We must obey God rather than men. The God of our fathers raised Jesus whom you put to death. . . We are witnesses of these things, and so is the Holy Spirit, whom God has given to all who obey him" (Ac 5:27-32).

This presence and power of the Holy Spirit manifest themselves naturally in them, whose witnessing brings them persecution or martyrdom. Taking his leave of the presbyters of Ephesus, St. Paul tells them: "I am going to Jerusalem, compelled by the Spirit, not knowing what will happen to me there; except that in every city the Holy Spirit warns me, saying that imprisonment and persecution are awaiting me" (Ac 20:22-23). And in the narrative of the martyrdom of St. Stephen, St. Luke writes of him: "He, being full of the Holy Spirit, looked up to heaven and saw the glory of God and Jesus standing at the right hand of God" (Ac 7:55).

The second power which Christ gave to build his Body is that of sanctifying men through the Sacraments. It is based on the words of our Lord such as these: "Baptize all nations;" "Do this in my memory;" "Whose sins you shall forgive, they are forgiven;" "You shall receive power when the Holy Spirit comes upon you, and you shall be witness for me;" and other commands of the Lord. By this power, the Church unites men gathering them in the Body of Christ, through the administration of these Sacraments. It is the Holy Spirit that works in these Sacraments. I will talk briefly about his unifying action through these Sacraments.

Of Baptism, St. Paul tells us: "We all were baptized in one Spirit into one body, whether Jew or Gentile, whether slave or free" (1 Cor 12:13). From Acts we can gather that the gift of the Holy Spirit conferred by the imposition of hands by the Apostles—in which consist the Sacrament of Confirmation—is accompanied normally by an outpouring of charisms, which according to St. Paul are granted by the Holy Spirit "for the construction of the Body of Christ." The Sacrament of Penance, where the Holy Spirit intervenes for "the remission of sins," is called the Sacrament of Reconciliation because the Holy Spirit reconciles the penitent not only with God but also with all the members of the Mystical Body, to which every sin brings harm. He thus reestablishes the bond of love with them, the bond that his sin had destroyed.

The Eucharist is the Sacrament of unity par *excellence*. "The cup of blessing that we bless, is it not the sharing of the blood of Christ? And the bread that we break, is it not the partaking of the body of the Lord?" asks St. Paul. Then he says: "Because the bread is one, we though many, are one body, all of us who partake of the one bread" (1 Cor 10:17-17). Every Christian who receives Communion united himself with Christ and with all the members of his Body. Now, it is the Holy Spirit, as we have seen, who brings about this union, as the new Eucharistic prayers declare. "May all of us who share in the body and blood of Christ be brought together in unity by the Holy Spirit" (*Eucharistic Prayer* II). "Grant that we, who are nourished by his body and blood, may be filled with his Holy Spirit and become one body, one spirit in Christ" (*Eucharistic Prayer* III).

The Sacrament of Marriage unites the spouses by making their union participate in the unity of Christ and the Church. "The two shall become one flesh," says St. Paul. "This is a great mystery. I mean in reference to Christ and his Church" (Ep 5:31-32). Now, as we have seen, it is the Holy Spirit, the bond of the Father and the Son, and the bond of Christ and the Church, who confers to the conjugal bond its solid indissolubility.

Through the Sacrament of Orders, the Holy Spirit making all priests participate in the unique Priesthood of Christ, unites them among themselves in the offering of his unique sacrifice and in the administration of the same Sacraments. And he unites them to the faithful. It seems that one could say of all priests what St. Paul said of the Apostles and Prophets: that they are the foundations of the structure of which "Christ Jesus is the chief cornerstone," and in which the faithful are built together into "a dwelling place for God in the Spirit" (Ep 2:20-22).

The third power or means with which the members of the hierarchy edify the Body of Christ is the power of guidance and direction of the faithful. It consists in giving Christians laws and directives, injunctions and advices, to lead them in the way of the commandments of the Lord, to help the faithful attain the end of the commandments: conformity to the image of Christ. This power is a remedy to egoism and self-sufficiency, to the spirit of indiscipline and to the dissensions and strife that flow from it, as well as to weakness and ignorance. This direction of the faithful in the ways of the commandments, under the authority of the same leader who represents effective unity, the bishop in his diocese, and the Pope in the whole Church, for conformity to the same model, unites them among themselves and to their Model. This power of the hierarchy brings about the growth and the construction of the Body of Christ, and is exercised under the action of the Holy Spirit, especially through the gift of counsel and the charism of discernment.

After conferring to his disciples these three powers, our Lord assured them that he would be with them "even to the cosummation of the world." He is with them conjointly with his Spirit, of whom he had said to them that he would be with them to teach them every truth. Such is the fundamental, essential role of the Holy Spirit in the Church. Without his presence and his action, the Church could not exist. Without his dynamic work, she would not live long, even less grow. The Holy Spirit gathers men under one head, Christ, to constitute of them his Body and to unite them to the Father, that the love with which the Father loves his Son be with them.

CHAPTER TEN

The Holy Spirit and the Charismatic Renewal

At the end of the preceding chapter, I have alluded to the passage in St. John where our Lord says that the Holy Spirit, whom the Father will send to the Church, will not be a temporary gift. Here is the whole passage:

> *I will ask the Father and he will give you another Advocate to dwell with you forever, the Spirit of truth whom the world cannot receive because it neither sees him nor knows him. But you shall know him, because he will dwell with you, and be in you.* (Jn 14:16-17).

Begun at Pentecost, the mission of the Holy Spirit in the Church and in the world will last until the end of time. "When the work which the Father had given the Son to do on earth," says Vatican II, "was accomplished, the Holy Spirit was sent on the day of Pentecost in order that He might forever sanctify the Church, and thus all believers would have access to the Father through Christ in the one Spirit" (*Lumen Gentium* #4).

Pentecost then continues. Our Lord never ceases sending from his Father the Holy Spirit, who carries on his work in the world and accomplishes the sanctification of all, as the 4th Eucharistic Prayer says. This work of love, inaugurated at the beginning of the evangelical preaching, and confirmed "by signs and wonders, and by manifold powers, and impartings of the Holy Spirit" (Heb 2:3-4), has never stopped. For twenty centuries, the Spirit has been building the Church, and spreading divine love in all the members of the Body of Christ, in order to gather together mankind in this One Body.

According to the needs and circumstances of each age, God gives the Church the means best adapted for the times. Today our world is marked by a profound and widespread crisis of faith, by a cooling off of many Christians, by the falling away of numerous priests and religious, by the collapse of morality in every domain of life, by the ravages of materialism and atheism and secularism, but also a world where many Christians, above all young Christians, feel the thirst for the absolute, the need of authenticity and personal experience, of simplicity and interior life, and at the same time yearn for tangible signs of communitarian life. At the same time God has caused to spring up a number of currents of grace destined to offer to contemporary Christians an increase of spiritual vitality. The so-called Charismatic Renewal is one of these currents of grace.

What is the Charismatic Renewal?

The "Charismatic Renewal," is also called, especially in France, "Renewal in the Spirit," or "Spiritual Renewal." Pope Paul VI spoke about this movement on several occasions. For example, during the Audience of October 16, 1974, he said:

> *It is absolutely necessary that the miracle of Pentecost continue throughout the history of the Church and the world. The gift of the Spirit must continue to be given in its two forms. This means, first, that the Spirit is given for the sanctification of men. This is the basic and indispensable gift, since by it man becomes an object of God's love (grace here "makes pleasing," gratum faciens, as the theologians put it). Second, the Spirit enriches men with special prerogatives we call "charisms" (or graces "given without merit," gratis datae), that are ordered to the good of the neighbor and especially to the good of the community of believers. There is much talk of charism today; it is a complex and sensitive subject. We can only desire a new outpouring not only of grace but of charism that are still being given to the Church of God in our day.*

In this spiritual renewal we may be seeing an answer to the prayer recommended to all Christians by Pope John XXIII, at the vigil of Vatican II: "Oh Holy Spirit, sent by the Father in the name of Jesus, you who help the Church with your presence and lead her infallibly, grant, we pray, to pour forth the fullness of your gifts upon the Ecumenical Council. Renew in our age your wonders, a new Pentecost."

Alluding to this prayer, Paul VI, in his Apostolic Exhortation of May 3, 1975, wrote the following:

> *We should see a prophetic intuition in our predecessor John XXIII, when he envisioned the fruit of the Council as a new Pentecost. We wish to place ourselves in the same perspective and expectation. . . Not that Pentecost has ever ceased to be actual throughout the history of the Church. Yet, so great are the needs and dangers of this century, so vast is the horizon of a humanity propelled to world-wide coexistence, and so manifest its powerlessness to realize it, that there is no salvation for it except in a new outpouring of the Gift of God. May the Creator Spirit come to renew the face of the earth!*

Before answering the question as to what is the Charismatic Renewal, I am going to give a summary of events that started the movement. (cf. Rene Laurentin, *Catholic Pentecostalism*, Doubleday, 1977). In August 1966, several lay professors of Duquesne University attended the Congress of the Cursillo movement. Fervent Catholics, they had already been involved in the liturgical, ecumenical and peace movements, as well as in other apostolates, but had felt disillusioned in all of them, feeling that something was missing in their Christian existence—something that would spark in them a total and joyous commitment to God.

At that Congress they met Steve Clark and Ralph Martin. Steve had been reading *The Cross and the Switchblade,* the autobiographical story of a Protestant pastor, who dedicated himself to work among deliquents and drug addicts in a dangerous Brooklyn neighborhood. In this book, the professors found that something they had failed to find in their previous apostolates: the Bible, the Holy Spirit and his mighty joyous charisms. They made the book the basis for their discussions and prayers, and tried to apply its lessons in their daily life. Sometime later, Ralph Keifer, another of the group, came across John Sherrill's *They Speak in Other Tongues*, which offered ways and means of attaining an experience of the Holy Spirit.

At the beginning of 1967, W. Lewis, an Episcopalian minister put them in touch with a woman who was involved in the charismatic movement. Four of the group took part in a prayer meeting on Friday, January 13. Of the four only Ralph returned the following week, bringing with him Patrick Bourgeois, another professor of the faculty of theology. At the end of the prayer and discussion, the two asked to receive the "baptism in the Holy Spirit." One group prayed over Ralph and imposed hands on him; another group did the same for Patrick.

"They simply asked me," Ralph Keifer writes, "to make an act of faith for the power of the Spirit to work in me. I prayed in tongues rather quickly. It was not a particularly soaring or spectacular thing at all. I felt a certain peace—at least a little prayerful—and truthfully rather curious as to where all this would lead."

In mid-February, about thirty students and professors, including Ralph Keifer, gathered at Duquesne University, for a weekend of prayer and reflection. On Saturday evening, at the time set for a birthday celebration, things suddenly began to happen, and many experienced the power and love of the Spirit; some spoke in tongues, others were favored with various other charisms, all felt sensibly the joyous love of the Holy Spirit.

The following account of Patti Gallagher, one of the students, portrays vividly what took place:

We were all tired from our day of prayer and reflection, and somewhat distraught. No one was very eager about setting up the birthday party for that evening. The Lord was at work in us, but we were not aware of it.

I wanted to shake off the feeling of apathy and to get something going, so I went to the chapel to see if any of the other students were there. I went in and knelt down, and began to tremble; I felt the presence of the Lord. I became

afraid, yet I wanted nothing so much as to stay there and pray. But I said to myself: "We've done enough praying today. It's time to celebrate our brother's birthday."
One of the students in the chapel said to me: "Patti, I don't understand it. Something's happening that we didn't plan." I answered: "I just want to pray." Then I improvised: "Lord, I don't know what you are asking, but I am ready."
Then I could feel God's love for me; I experienced it. I was prostrate on the ground, overwhelmed by the "foolishness" of this love. I knew no theology, I had never gone to Catholic schools, but as I lay prostrate there I understood Augustine's words: "Lord, you made us for yourself; only in you will we find peace." I realized that the others in the chapel were having the same experience.

At the same time, in a room upstairs, Ralph Keifer was praying with Paul Grey and Maryanne Springle, an engaged couple, who had expressed the wish to him of receiving the "baptism in the Spirit." They received it and spoke in tongues. Patti, herself, received this charism a few days later. On that weekend dates the beginning of the charismatic renewal among Catholics. A similar event took place at the University of Notre Dame, on the weekend of March 4-5.

Since the movement got its inspiration from Pentecostalism, which had its beginnings among a group of believers, led by a Methodist pastor, Charles Parham, it seems profitable to touch briefly on what happened among them. I shall do so by quoting the following from Laurentin:

"The best-qualified witness is Agnes Ozman, who was the first to have the specifically pentecostal experience of "baptism in the Spirit" and "speaking in tongues." According to her, the event occurred during a vigil, at 11 P.M., January 1, 1901.

"It happened in a Topeka, Kansas, house where Charles Parham, Methodist pastor, had established a Bible school. He and his students were deeply impressed by the contrast between the gloominess of the present-day Church and the vibrant life of the early Church as described in the Acts of the Apostles: a bracing, joyous, energetic life that was permeated by the breath of the Spirit. How do we account for the disappearance of those charisms in which the first

Christians saw the manifestation of the Spirit, especially the gift of tongues of which Acts speaks? It was not a satisfactory answer to say that these were temporary, exceptional gifts meant only for the period when the Church was being founded, or, to switch to St. John Chrysostom's image, that they were "gifts for the period of engagement" and lost their meaning once the marriage was under way. The Bible, after all, gives no hint that the gifts were to be temporary, while the Church history shows them being given again at moments when Christianity was really vital, and especially at times of change.

"At this point in his study and reflection Pastor Parham held a prayer vigil on New Year's Eve (December 31, 1900). The next day one of the students, Agnes Ozman (later Mrs. La Berge) felt impelled to ask the pastor to lay his hands on her head, as described in the New Testament, so that she might receive the gift of the Spirit. The pastor hesitated, then agreed.

"It was as though rivers of living water were proceeding from my inmost being," she said later on. The words echoing in her memory here were those of John: "Let the man come and drink who believes in me. As Scripture says: 'From his breast shall flow fountains of living water.'" The evangelist then comments on these words of Jesus: "He was speaking of the Spirit which those who believed in him were to receive" (Jn 7:38-39).

"Agnes began to speak in strange tongues . . . On the following days other members of the Bible school had the same experience" (Laurentin, *op. cit.*, pp. 18-19).

Rejected by the Methodist Church, where it had been born, isolated during a long period of time, Pentecostalism began to interest traditional Protestant Churches: from 1958 the Episcopal, in 1962 the Lutheran and in 1967 the Presbyterian Church. In the same year, as we have seen, Catholic neo-Pentacostalism or the charismatic renewal, was born at Duquesne University. Soon after, a number of priests joined it, and even bishops became interested. The rapid spread of the movement is seen in the increasing number of people who have attended the annual meeting at the University of Notre Dame. In fact, in 1967, some 90 persons were present; in 1974, seven years later, about 30,000 gathered together. From the United States the movement crossed over into Canada. A spontaneous meeting in Quebec, in June 1974, brought together over 8,000 people. Laurentin describes the charismatic renewal in Puerto Rico as "a tidal wave." At the end of 1971, it had its beginnings in various parts of France.

I think it is useful to mention some of the movement's most obvious dangers. Laurentin lists the following: fundamentalism, or the "naively literal, material and 'obvious' interpretation of Scripture;" subjectivism; illuminism, or "direct communication with God, the expectation of light without making free use of one's intelligence;" emotionalism, sentimentality; and spiritual gluttony (*op.cit.*, pp. 163 ff.).

The greatest danger is that the movement may become a *sect*. However, the charismatics want it to be considered not as another organization, with its own structures, hierarchy and particular task— another "small group movement," interested in the renovation of the Church. They see it as a collective outburst, sparked by the re-discovery of the Holy Spirit and his action—an experience lived in a prayer meeting and, more often, after a special outpouring of the Spirit, in view of the building of the Body of Christ. Thus far, as Laurentin says: "The charismatic movement, unlike many other small group movements, has in fact been marked by a firm attachment to the Church as to a home and a foundation" (*op. cit.*, p. 164).

I'm going to talk about the two essential elements of the charismatic movement: the prayer meeting and the "outpouring of the Spirit."

The charismatic prayer meeting is a gathering of Christians who have become conscious of the presence of the risen Lord, who once said: "If two of you shall agree on earth about anything at all for which they ask, it shall be done for them by my Father in heaven. For where two or three are gathered together for my sake, there am I in the midst of them" (Mt 18:19-20).

The first characteristic of a charismatic gathering is then a vivid faith in the presence of the Lord Jesus Christ, who is there, in their midst and in each of them, and in whose name these Christians gather "to pray steadfastly" as the primitive Christian community were wont to. (Ac 2:42).

The number of participants in the meetings varies from several to several hundred persons, consisting of lay people of all conditions and ages, many young people, priests and religious, even bishops.

Waiting for the meeting to begin, the new members are welcomed; all seek to know each other better. At the end of the prayer, those who came for the first time are invited to meet again to learn more about the movement. Another group gathers to prepare those who want to receive "the outpouring of the Spirit." Also, the charismatics gather once a month, on a weekend day, to receive doctrinal teaching from a theologian.

First of all, a meeting of this type differs from groups that meditate in common, or discuss the evangelical message. It also differs from a liturgical action, whose unfolding is determined by precise rules, whether it be the Eucharist or the recitation of the Hours of the Office. Regularly the meeting lasts for about an hour and a half to two hours. Sometimes it may last four or five hours. The participants place themselves in concentric circles around a Bible or an icon or both.

It is of utmost importance that one come to these meetings, feeling spiritually poor, and ready and willing to surrender his *ego* or his "me," a voluntarist "me" that wants to do things or say something by oneself. In other words, a state of spiritual detachment is necessary—a disposition which will let one experience the truth of the words of St. Paul: "We do not know what we should pray for as we ought" (Rm 8:26).

The meeting often begins with a joyous, thankful song that intends to express the joy of finding oneself among brothers and sisters in Jesus Christ, all happily praying together. Then the leader of the meeting delivers a few words of advice to the participants in order that the prayer meeting may unfold in due order, in docility to the Spirit, through whom Jesus will pray in each, and in openness to one another. The leader then guides it discreetly, orients it, pays attention to its unfolding, and finally brings it to an end.

The leader is usually a lay person who is chosen because he or she is endowed with the charism of "presiding." The leader does not direct the prayer, but enjoys, however, a certain role of authority. He may, for instance, intervene "to break" a too great exaltation, to re-orient the meeting toward the praising and thanksgiving of the Lord, or to a greater silence and openness to each other. This openness permits the prayer to be the prayer of all. The participants must feel that they are taking part in a communitarian prayer, where each carries and is carried by the others. To attain this it is necessary that the prayer of each be, above all, an attitude of docile listening to the Spirit, who himself prays in each and who shapes the prayer of the meeting. The prayer then is not really uttered by any of the participants, but should be received as a gift of God, a prayer of the Spirit, who dwells in us and makes us cry: *Abba*! Beloved Father!

In some groups, a brief teaching is given in the course of the meeting either by a cleric or by a lay person.

Though order and unity prevail in the unfolding of the meeting, there is also a great spontaneity. Each participant may freely intervene, either to thank the Lord with an extemporaneous prayer, or to praise him by reading a psalm, or to proclaim his wonders, or by intoning a hymn. This may be dollowed by a deep silence. Then the prayer itself may start again after the reading of an appropriate scriptural passage, as St. Paul recommends to the Colossians: "Let the word of Christ dwell in you abundantly" (3:16). Sometimes a verse from the sacred text or just a word from it sets in motion a unanimous praise in which each expresses his gratitude and wonder, either in words said in an undertone, or in a song "in tongues" of singular beauty. This chant, similar to the tones of an organ, develops harmoniously and rhythmically, finally becomes a song that wells up from the depths of hearts, like the inspired chants of which St. Paul speaks, for example, in Colossians: "In all wisdom teach and admonish one another by psalms, hymns and spiritual songs, singing in your hearts to God" (3:16). Sometimes, a participant "sings in tongues," all alone by himself, either to exalt the glory of God, to praise and thank him, or and also to utter a "prophecy." A "prophecy" may be uttered in the language of the participants and without being sung.

In general, one is struck by the atmosphere of fervor, youthfulness, fraternal love and free spontaneity which prevails in these meetings. This atmosphere does not fail sometimes to affect favorably unbelievers or persons in search of the faith, who have come to be present at these meetings. Frequently these meetings end by participation in the Eucharist Assembly. Far from substituting themselves to the liturgical assemblies, charismatic meetings lead to a better participation in them.

What unites the members of the charismatic movement is the discovery of the Lord living in them. All their prayers and songs are the tangible and spontaneous manifestation of the presence of Jesus Christ. Now, this personal and totally new awareness is the work of the Holy Spirit, the Great Unknown, the Great Unrecognized, whose discovery and experience is being made once more among the charismatics.

This experiential awareness of the presence of the Holy Spirit, acting in them, has given the label of "charismatics" to the members of the movement. However, this label does not mean at all that a sort of monopoly is being given only to a number of Christians of what belongs to the whole Church and to each of the faithful. The "charismatics" then do not constitute a superior category of Christians—an *elite*. All Christians are charismatics because the Church whose members they are part of is wholly charismatic, for she is animated by the Spirit, who is building unceasingly the Body of Christ. If the movement is called charismatic it is because it leads "to a higher and conscious tension, the charismatic dimension inherent in the Church" as Cardinal Suenens has said.

What distinguishes the "charismatics" from other Christians is then a more vivid consicousness of the fundamental reality necessarily common to all Christians. It is also the fact that in the meetings of the members of the charismatic movement there take place charismatic phenomena, in the strict meaning of extraordinary events, such as "speaking in tongues," the "prophecies," and the gift of healing. The label of "charismatic" has the advantage of "putting in relief the full reintegration of charism in the 'normal' life of the Church, both local and universal," as *Lumen Vitae* puts it.

In the charismatic renewal, in fact, there are taking place the charisms which flourished in the primitive Church, as Pope Paul VI pointed out, in his Allocution of December 21, 1973: "The fresh breath of the Spirit has come to awaken latent energies within the Church, to stir up dormant charisms, and to infuse a sense of vitality and joy. It is that sense of vitality and joy which makes the Church youthful and relevant in every age, and prompts her to joyously proclaim her eternal message to each new epoch."

The charisms occur generally after the so-called "outpouring of the Spirit," through which some members of the movement opened themselves totally to the action of the Holy Spirit.

The "outpouring of the Spirit," the second basic element of the charismatic renewal is, of course, not a sacrament. It differs then essentially from Baptism and Confirmation. That is the reason why the term "baptism in the Spirit," used in classical Pentecostalism to designate the outpouring, is rejected by many Catholic members of the movement, especially in France. For it may lead one to believe that it is a question of a sacrament, of another baptism, and consequently the Sacrament of Baptism is deficient and that a second baptism is necessary.

The "outpouring of the Spirit" is not even a rite properly speaking but a twofold step in view of an intervention of the Spirit in the life of the person who asks for the outpouring.

It is, first of all, a personal step of *conversion* and of *spiritual renewal*. It is "what has been traditionally called "conversion," by which is meant a "second conversion," that is, the act by which a Christian effectively turns to the living God," as Laurentin rightly describes it (cf. *op. cit.*, p. 43).

When one receives Baptism, he puts on "the new man," according to St. Paul's expression (Col 3:10). He is radically transformed on the *plane of being*: he becomes a son of God; he can say with St. Paul: "It is now no longer I that live, but Christ who lives in me" (Gal 2:19-20). It remains for one to become on the *plane of conduct* what one is on the plane of being: he must be transformed morally. This moral transformation lasts the whole of one's life. The new man, as St. Paul says, "does not cease being renewed unto perfect knowledge according to the image of his Creator" (Col 3:10); "the inner man is being renewed day by day" (2 Cor 4:16).

It is in view of this unceasing renewal that the "outpouring of the Spirit" is asked. I have already shown in what, according to St. Paul, this work of conversion and moral transformation consists of (cf. Chapter 8). I have shown how we must acquire the very morals and manners of God, by becoming conformed to the image of his Son, and how we must imitate God by the following of Jesus Christ, as becomes well-beloved children of God.

The member of the charismatic meeting who asks for the "outpouring of the Spirit" is a Christian who, confronted with this work of continuous renewal, a most difficult work far exceeding the forces of our nature, becomes aware of his weakness and helplessness. He realizes that holiness or the imitation of Christ is not a perfection that one attains by *his own will* or by the sheer force of ascetic work. Having then experienced the truth of the words of the Lord, "Without me you can do nothing" (Jn 15:5), St. Paul says: "I can do all things in him who strengthens me" (Phil 4:13). In the light of the teaching of the Apostle, he understands that he who strengthens is Christ working through his Spirit. "If by the Spirit you put to death the deeds of the flesh, you will live. For, whoever are led by the Spirit of God they are the sons of God" (Rm 8:13-14).

He resolves then to place his trust in the power of the Spirit, following St. Paul's recommendation to the Galatians: "If we live by the Spirit, by the Spirit let us also walk" (5:25). Consequently, he renounces his *voluntarism*, which alas motivates too many Christians, and he surrenders totally to the action of the Spirit for the work of his sanctification. However, he does not fall into a sort of quietism, knowing well that faith in the power of the Spirit does not do away with the necessity of asceticism, but he rightly puts ascetic efforts in their proper or secondary place. He can then in all truth say with St. Paul: "By the grace of God I am what I am" (1 Cor 15:10). He takes pride not in himself and in his efforts, but takes pride in the Lord (1 Cor 1:29-31). He can thus become "a praise of the glory of his grace" (Ep 1:16).

To implement his resolve, he asks for the "outpouring of the Spirit." This outpouring may take place during or at the end of the prayer meeting. However, it usually takes place in a small group. The petitioner expresses to the Lord his desire to belong more fully to him, to surrender wholly to the Holy Spirit, so that he may be freed from everything which is an obstacle to the Spirit's sanctifying action, and that having gotten rid of his selfishness, sensuality, fears and laziness, he may let the Spirit work more freely and powerfully to renew him according to the image of the Son of God, that he may become and act more and more like a child of God, a witness of the trinitarian and fraternal love before men.

The "outpouring of the Spirit" is secondly a communitarian step. All the members of the group pray God to grant the petition of their brother or sister, trusting on the promise of the Lord "If two of you shall agree on earth about anything at all for which they ask, it shall be done for them by my Father in heaven. For where two or three are gathered together for my sake, there am I in the midst of them."

The "outpouring of the Spirit" is not an ecstatic experience. Its goal is to let the Holy Spirit, received in Baptism and Confirmation, produce the fruits of the two Sacraments, more effectively by becoming more aware of them. These Sacraments do not work automatically. The powers and the gifts which they communicate have need to be exercised. The Holy Spirit is the soul who animated the Body of Christ and each of its members. For many Christians the work of the Holy Spirit is obstructed by obstacles of all sorts. Many baptized and confirmed Christians have indeed the Holy Spirit in fullness, but this "Living Water," that is the Spirit, is in them as a sealed source. The "outpouring of the Spirit" proves a most effective means to unseal the divine source and to take away the obstacles which impede the "water" to flow to make glad and more fruitful the everyday life of the believers. The action of the Spirit awakens in the Christiam dormant powers, and activates dormant charisms. By this action, the Holy Spirit renews and transforms into an image of Christ the Christian who asks for the outpouring.

The prayer with which the charismatic gathering supports the petition is accompanied habitually by a gesture used both in the Old and New Testaments, namely, the laying on of hands. We find in the Gospels, that our Lord imposed his hands on the children to bless them and on the sick to cure them. In the Acts of the Apostles, we see the Apostles laying their hands on the newly-baptized to invoke the Holy Spirit to come upon them; and a simple Christian, Ananias, laying his hands on St. Paul that he might receive his sight and the Holy Spirit. Our Lord himself told all believers in him "to lay hands on the sick and they shall get well." The laying of hands is also used in the official Ordination of the presbyterate, and on the appointment of the seven deacons for the service of the tables.

The gesture of the laying on of hands used in the charismatic movement is connected with this tradition. As Laurentin points out: "Usually it is an act of the whole group; is done at the individual's request, and is accompanied by common prayer for the individual's need. He may be seeking an outpouring of the Spirit, a grace of light or strength for the apostolate or in some difficult situation, a healing, and so on. The laying on of hands is a concrete, sensible expression of solidarity, this last being highly esteemed in the charismatic movement" (*op. cit.*, pp. 56 ff.).

The laying on of hands is not a sacramental rite as in the Sacraments of Confirmation and Holy Orders. Yet less is it a magical gesture which would transmit I don't know what powers one has in one's possession. It is a gesture which expresses visibly the solidarity of the charismatic group, and their desire that their prayer be directed toward the petitioner who is seeking help. So many hands imposed on him or extended toward him will not fail to move and comfort him, while all the voices join themselves in a fervent prayer and in joyous songs.

This laying on of hands seems to me to have another significance. This gesture is in the very logic of the concrete reality of the mystery of the Incarnation. It is by the intermediary of his humanity, of his soul *and of his body*, that our Lord accomplished his salvific work. Ascending to the heavens, he continues this work through the intermediary of his extended humanity, or by his "Body which is the Church" (Col 1:24), of which all Christians are members. By their intermediary, he lays on hands as he did on the sick and sinful in Palestine. It is then by contact with what has been called his "additional humanity" that he communicates his graces and his gifts. The new ritual of the Sacrament of Reconciliation provides that the confessor can lay his hands on the penitents that he absolves.

The imposition of hands in the charismatic movement means then the orientation of the prayer of the community, in a manifestation of solidarity, toward the petitioner seeks to implore the Lord to accept his consent to let the Spirit flow in him, to let himself be led, acted on, renewed and transformed by him, and to grant him the necessary graces to hold fast to his consent. It also means the communication that the Holy Spirit makes to him of his grace and gifts.

The Effects of the "Outpouring Of The Spirit."

The "charismatics" assert that the "outpouring of the Spirit" on them causes them to live their Christian life under the power of the Holy Spirit: with more vitality, facility, interiority and joy. This spiritual renewal is brought about through the following effects, either at the very moment of the event, several days or even several months afterwards.

The *first* effect is the growth of the divine life in Christians, thanks to a better exercise of the theological virtues of faith, hope and love. This growth is set in motion by the discovery, or by a more vivid awareness, of the presence in Christians of the divine Persons, of the God of Love, of the Holy Spirit especially. This awareness leads to more personal and interior praying to the Father, or to the Son, or to the Holy Spirit, or to the Father in the Son through the Spirit. Contrary to what certain critics think of the movement, the prayer does not lack the Trinitarian dimension. Indeed, one could fear that the discovery of the Spirit would make the "charismatics" relegate in the shadow both the Father and the Son. It hasn't happened thus. On the contrary, the Holy Spirit makes them better know and love the Father and the Son; he effects their identification to the well-beloved Son, and he makes them experience the filial love of God, as St. Paul says: "The proof that we are sons is that God has sent the Spirit of his Son into our hearts, crying, *Abba,* Father" (Gal 4:6).

Moreover, by reminding them, that they have here on earth "no permanent city, but we seek for the city that is to come" (Heb 13:14), the Spirit makes them desire the Return of the Lord—now visibly absent—and he makes the Church sigh for her Spouse, according to the words of St. John: "The Spirit and the bride say: 'Come!' (Rv 22:17). While rejoicing already for his mystical coming in each of them, they wait for his final coming in glory, for his *Parousia,* by repeating with St. John: "Come, Lord Jesus!" (Rv 22:20).

Secondly, the Holy Spirit makes the "charismatics" experience fraternal love. He establishes among them a communion in Jesus Christ, that makes them transparent one to another. He makes them love as Jesus loves them, of a love true, sincere, disinterested, effective, warm, human. He simplifies their relations to one another by doing away with barriers of all sorts, with distrust and prejudices. By giving them a renewed sense of the presence in them of God and his Christ, he creates among them personal relations of greater depth. He sets up among them bonds of another order, the bonds of a family in Christ Jesus. He banishes loneliness and isolation and grants them the joy of being united in the One Body of Christ: to be brothers and sisters in him, to the point that many among them greet each "mutually with a holy kiss" (cf. Rm 16:16; 1 Cor 15:20; 2 Cor 13:12; 1 P 5:14).

This fraternal love, far from attaching them to only the charismatic groups, opens them to all people without distinction of race, nor of religion, nor of class; and it puts them at the service of all. They practice fraternal love that one can truly say of them not only, "See how they love each other," but also, "See how they love!"

That they may be able to love each other as brothers and sisters, serve each other and to witness Christ and his Gospel, The Holy Spirit seems to be instilling in the hearts of a certain number of "charismatics" the desire to live together. In France, for example, their prayer groups have been developing into communitarian living, a community of prayer, where the praising and giving thanks to the Lord prevails. Small communities are being formed, where stronger bonds are established: a strong mutual commitment and a greater solidarity and communication.

Thanks to the charismatic groups which are beginning to penetrate parishes the Holy Spirit is renewing and vivifying the liturgical assemblies. By spreading his charisms among the faithful, he is enlisting them for the manifold work of the pastoral ministry, confiding to each a greater share for the construction of that portion of the Body of Christ which is the parish.

A third effect of the "outpouring of the Spirit" is attraction for prayer, for the prayer of praise and thanksgiving, in a special way.

It can be said safely that few are the Christians who give proper thanks to God; even fewer are those who praise him. When people pray, it is first of all and most often, if not only and always, to ask God for things. Of course, it is not forbidden to ask; on the contrary it is even recommended. However, Sacred Scripture and the Liturgy invite us mainly to praise and thank God. St. Paul asks this kind of prayer invariably: "Be filled with the Spirit, speaking to one another in psalm and hymns and spiritual songs, singing and making melody in your hearts to the Lord, giving thanks always for all things in the name of our Lord Jesus Christ to God the Father" (Ep 5:18-19). In the same Epistle he tells the Ephesians: "You were sealed with the Holy Spirit of the promise, who is the pledge of our inheritance, for a redemption of possession, for the praise of his glory" (1:13-14). The same declaration comes forth from St. Peter: "You are a chosen race, a royal priesthood, a holy nation, a purchased people; that you may proclaim the perfection of him who has called you out of darkness into his marvellous light" (1 P 2:9).

As for the Liturgy, it draws its inspiration from these scriptural teachings and recommendations in its celebration. The faithful are enjoined to say or to chant: "We give thanks to God;" and "Praise to you, Lord Jesus." But it seems that very few are fully aware why they are thanking or praising God and Jesus Christ. Now, the "outpouring of the Spirit" makes those so favored sensitive to these two types of prayer, by precisely making them aware of the reasons why they should praise and thank the Lord.

The "outpouring" makes them sensitive to giving thanks to God because the Holy Spirit himself is the Prayer of Thanksgiving *par excellence,* he being the grateful love of Christ for his Father. Having for his mission to teach us all the truth, the Spirit also makes the "charismatics" who surrender to him to comprehend better the wonders that the Holy Trinity has done for humanity in general: Creation, Incarnation, Redemption, the Filial Adoption, the Eucharist; and the spiritual wonders done for them in particular.

The "out pouring" also makes them sensitive to the praising of God because the Holy Spirit, who "scrutinizes the deep things of God" (1 Cor 2:10-11), makes them discover the very life of the divine Persons: the plenitude of love that is lived in the bosom of the Blessed Trinity, where he himself is the very communion of the love of the Father and the Son. The Spirit, moreover, makes them perceive better the invisible perfections of God through his wondrous works in history: his beauty, might, holiness, justice, mercy, faithfulness, goodness, tenderness and so on. This excellent awareness that the Spirit imparts to them, of the Trinitarian mystery of love and of the divine perfections, fills them with joy and makes them exalt, magnify and glorify God, his Christ and their common Spirit. And from the hearts of the "charismatics" there spring up a joyous and toally free prayer of praise.

The prayer of thanksgiving and of praise often blend together, one into another, and express themselves through a song, sometimes through a prayer "in tongues," uttered or sung either individually or collectively—sometimes intelligible language finds itself incapable of expressing the wonder and gratitude of the human spirit when seized by the Holy Spirit.

These two forms of prayer often work healings and interior transformations. This is true, above all, of the prayer of praise. To praise, in fact, is to *decentralize* oneself in order to *centralize* oneself on God, on Christ and on the Spirit: consequently to come out of oneself, of one's problems and lonelines, to forget one's miseries and faults, worries and cares, in order to turn oneself entirely toward God, to give him thanks for his immense glory, unfailing mercy, to become ecstatic before his eternal youth and beauty, to contemplate the plenitude of life and love which is his, and to take part in it. One's heart then finds trust, calm and joy. That is why, thanks to the "outpouring of the Spirit" one succeeds in thanking and praising God at all times and in every circumstance, even during one's worst trials. These prayers indeed, are inspired by an unconditional faith in the love of the Lord, which the Spirit gives to one. And one puts an absolute trust in God's paternal providence, in his gracious plans, even though one fails to understand his ways, since, as Isaias said, *his ways are not our ways.*

To be sure, the prayer of thanksgiving and praise presupposes the prayer of adoration to which they lead; and they do not at all exclude the prayer of petition, nor that of intercession, nor that of repentance, as the following passage of St. Paul shows: "With all prayer and supplications pray at all times in the Spirit, and therein be vigilant in all perseverance and supplication for all the saints, and for me" (Ep 6:18). However, he tells the Philippians that "In every prayer and supplication with thanksgiving let your petitions be made known to God" (4:6).

On account of his stress on prayer, especially on thanksgiving and praise, the fear could be expressed that the charismatic movement may become an escape from the world, a flight from social commitments. To have the faith, as Cardinal Suenens remarks, "is not only to raise our eyes toward God, to contemplate him, it is also to look at the earth but with the eyes of Christ. The danger of a withdrawal on oneself or on the group does not escape the attention of those responsible for the movement." On the contrary, they alert constantly the "charismatics" to it, by reminding them that "communion in prayer must naturally issue in the great fraternal communion of man, with its social and political implications" in order to promote the integral liberation and development of humanity.

Another effect of the "outpouring of the Spirit" is the discovery of the Bible, or a greater attraction and love for the Word of God, and a more diligent reading of Scripture. "Charismatics" delight in it, nourish themselves with it, feed their faith and prayer with it. All this leads to the desire to know the Bible better through a deeper study of it under the action of the Holy Spirit—whose mission is to teach us all profitable things, to make us remember everything that Jesus said and did, and to arrive at all the truth. This study makes them avoid a fundamentalist position, or a "naively literal, material and 'obvious' interpretation of Scripture," as Laurentin puts it. Some members of the movement carry with them a copy of the New Testament or the whole Bible.

Yet another effect of the "outpouring" is attachment to the Church. One would have feared in this too that the personal experience of the Spirit would lead the "charismatics" to detach themselves from the *institutional* Church. The contrary seems to have taken place—thus far at least. An observer wrote in the periodical *Fetes et Saisons* that the charismatic experience "is leading to a better understanding of the Church. The young are returning to her because they are becoming aware that the Church is both charismatic and institutional. If she is only an institution she dies; if she is only charismatic she becomes insane."

This better understanding of the Church as an institution animated by the Spirit, as the domicile of the Spirit, leads the "charismatics" to a filial love for this Church, to a greater docility to her teachings, to a more diligent practice of the Sacrament of Reconciliation, a Sacrament better understood thanks to a deeper perception of the sense of sin, stemming from a greater comprehension of the sense of God, of Christ and of man—all gifts of the Holy

Spirit. The "charismatics" participate in the Eucharistic celebrations more frequently, and seem to be showing a more authentic devotion to Mary, having discovered her true and singular role in the Church and in the salvific plans of God. The members of the movement are more fully aware that in the institutional Church there are many things that are not vivified by "the living waters of the Spirit"; however, they do not seem to react with bitterness or discouragement, nor with sectarian pride.

This greater attachment to the Church does not set them apart from other Christian groups. Ecumenism is the work of the Holy Spirit, the Spirit of truth, love and unity. Now, thanks to the charismatic renewal, which is spreading in all Churches, there is taking place in them a powerful convergent action in the One Spirit. Vatican II invited Catholics "not to forget that what is accomplished by the grace of the Holy Spirit among our separated brothers can contribute to our edification" (*Unitatis redintegratio, IV).* The charismatic renewal has led Christians of different communions to share, in meetings with Catholics, the experience of prayer and spiritual renewal, in faith and love. If these ecumenical meetings are conducted with good pastoral orientation, they can bring a significant contribution to the cause of Christian unity.

The "outpouring of the Spirit" is stirring up also the desire to announce the Gospel, to witness for Christ, dead and risen for us, to proclaim the wondrous works of God, as the Apostles did, to share with others the "glad tidings" brought to us by Jesus Christ: the love of the Father for all. Charismatics say: "We cannot but speak of what we have seen and heard" (Ac 4:20). The charismatic renewal is giving back to the Holy Spirit the primordial role that is his in this work of evengelization.

"There will never be any possibility of evangelization without the action of the Holy Spirit," declared Pope Paul VI, in his Apostolic Exhortation, *Evangelii nuntiandi,* of December 8, 1975. And he added:

> *The most refined preparation of the evangelist brings no fruit without the Holy Spirit. Without him, the most convincing dialectics is powerless on the human spirit. Without him, the most elaborated sociological or psy-*

chological schemes prove themselves quickly bereft of value. At this moment, we live in the Church in times that are favorable to the Spirit. Everywhere people seek to know him better, as Scripture reveals him. They are happy to put themselves under his inspiration. They gather together around him. They want to be led by him. Now if the Spirit has a most eminent place in the whole life of the Church, it is even greater in her mission of evangelization. It is not by accident that the grand beginnings of the evangelization of the world took place on the morning of Pentecost, under the breath of the Spirit.

In the same Exhortation, the Pope said: "The 1974 Synod of Bishops, which insisted strongly on the role of the Holy Spirit on the work of evangelization, expressed also the wish that pastors and theologians—and we will say, also the faithful marked with the seal of the Spirit study better the nature and the mode of the action of the Holy Spirit in evangelization today."

What the charismatic renewal in a special way, is discovering in the field of evangelization, is faith in the power of God, working through signs and wonders with which "God approved" his Christ, and which our Lord himself told the Apostles would accompany the proclamation of the Gospel, signs and wonders which were to be manifestations of his Spirit: "Go in the whole world and preach the gospel to every creature. . . And these signs shall attend those who believe: in my name they shall cast out devils; they shall speak in new tongues; they shall take up serpents; and if they drink any deadly thing, it shall not hurt them; they shall lay hands upon the sick and they shall get well" (Mk 16:16-18).

For various historical reasons, more or less valid, the miraculous manifestations which indeed took place among primitive Christians were set aside as appropriate only for the first generations of Christians. Moreover, charismatic gifts, such as "speaking in tongues," and "prophecies," were looked upon with suspicion and fear by the leaders of the Church through the centuries, especially since the condemnation of Montanism, in the 2d century A.D. In fairness, we must say that these "strange" wonders can be abused and can lead to a sectarian spirit of elitism and self-righteousness.

However, miracles never ceased to take place in the Church: and today she is welcoming the reappearance of the charismatic wonders.

If the charismatic renewal is truly the work of the Holy Spirit, then soon the preacher of the Gospel in the Church will not be content to proclaim the Word of God "in words only," according to St. Paul's expression. And he will ask the Lord to accompany his preaching "in power also, and in the Holy Spirit and in much fulness" (1 Th 1:3-5). To effectively proclaim the Gospel, the contemporary preachers will imitate the first Christian preachers, who prayed the Lord thusly: "Lord, grant to thy servants to speak thy word with all boldness, while thou stretchest forth thy hand to cures and signs and wonders to be brought by the name of thy holy servant Jesus" (Ac 4:29-30).

Before speaking more about the charisms, alluded to in the above passage from Acts, I should like to mention briefly yet another effect of the "outpouring of the Spirit."

Following this "outpouring," frequently people troubled by various ills experience an amazing liberation from these ills. The more vivid awareness of the presence of God, the surrender to the transforming action of the Holy Spirit brings liberation from various forms of interior slavery: vices, disordered sexuality, eroticism, violence, etc.; from exterior slavery: alcoholism, drug addiction, tyrannnic habit of tobacco, etc. People certify as being freed from certain psychological blocs: anxieties, anguish, obsession of suicide, pathological scruples, varied complexes, etc.

On the phenomenon of charismatic liberation, Laurentin writes the following:

> *The phenomena associated with Pentecost (the original Pentecost and its renewals today) imply, by any accounting, a liberation of psychic resources that are still not very well known. This liberation, moreover, has a negative and a positive side.*
>
> *The* negative *side of the phenomenon consists in the elimination of rigidities, inhibitions, and superstructures that dam up vital energies, both spiritaul and simply human. To express this aspect of their experience, people use various images. There is a thaw; the ice breaks up and the waters flow. A wall is razed; the interior defenses are dismantled*

and the subject moves out of his imprisoning egoism into contact with God and his fellow men.

The positive *side (inseparable from the negative) consists in the liberation and fruitful exercise of resources hitherto unknown or inoperative; this in turn helps to moral and physical balance. The energies liberated are applied to prayer, service and the apostolate.* (op. cit., pp. 150 ff.).

"Speaking in Tongues" and Other Charisms

After having been rare for many centuries, New Testament charisms have made their reappearance in these latter years, especially among the members of the charismatic movement.

Here I am going to discuss two of these charisms, the two which in a most extraordinary manner manifest the presence of the Lord working through his Spirit: the gift of *tongues* and the gift of *prophecy*. Then I will finish this study with a discussion of another charism, which is of the utmost importance: the gift of discernment.

From numerous passages of the New Testament, it can be seen that the gift of tongues," or *glossolalia,* is one of a number of charisms given by the Holy Spirit to attest or confirm the witnessing that our Lord demanded of his disciples. The *glossolalia* is the one charism which is the most talked about and looked upon with great suspicion by those who are not members of the charismatic movement. And yet, "charismatics" do not give too much importance to this phenomenon. It does take place, however; and they take their stand upon Scripture and Tradition to justify its existence.

In fact, our Lord himself told his Apostles about this gift (cf. Mk 16:15-18); St. Paul mentions the phenomenon several times (cf. 1 Cor 12:30; 13:1; 14:2, 39); the Book of Acts does the same (cf. 2:4, 11; 10:46; 19:6).

The charism of tongues has prayer, especially the prayer of praise, for its essential function (cf. Ac 2:11; 10:46). It is one of the ways the Holy Spirit prays in us, leading us to praise the wonders that God has done for us, among which, the marvellous work of our renewal by the Spirit, gained for us by the Resurrection of Jesus Christ.

There are two forms of this praying in tongues: collective and individual.

The most widespread is the collective form, of which I spoke earlier in this book. Laurentin writes that "it can even become a mass occurence, as at the Notre Dame meeting of June 1974, which thirty thousand attended." He says: "At one point a harmonious murmuring arose from the whole assembly; nothing harsh or cacophonous about it, and at moments it was quite beautiful" (op. cit., p. 63 ff.). The phenomenon "usually occurs at a time when prayer is more intense and seems to be poised between silence and speech." One cannot find words to celebrate the wonders of God and to thank him. And what follows "is less a 'speaking' than a chant or lyric modulation in praise of the 'marvels of God.' "

The second is individual. Only one speaks in tongues, while the others listen in silence. He speaks or chants by uttering syllables which succeed one another without being articulated in phrases, which however, as Laurentin points out, "possess a degree of coherence and phonetic clarity" (*op. cit.,* p. 64). The speaker does not understand what he is saying or chanting, but he remains master of himself, being able to begin or not, continue or stop; he is not then either in a trance or in ecstasy. He utters or chants praises in a language, which neither he nor those who listen understand. In this case, as St. Paul says (1 Cor 14:2), "he does not speak to men but to God;" "he edifies himself," since "his spirit prays" (14:4) "he praises God and gives thanks to him" (14:16-17). This being so, it is preferable that he who prays in tongues do it "to himself and to God" (14:28).

As a matter of fact, he does not edify the assembly, for "no one," says St. Paul, "understands, as he is speaking mysteries in his spirit" (1 Cor 14:2), unless he can interpret so that the assembly may receive edification" (14:5). The Apostle adds, "let him who speaks in a tongue pray that he may interpret" (14:13). Most of the times, the interpretation is given by another person, whom the Holy Spirit has gifted with this particular charism: the interpretation of tongues (12:10). Thanks to this charism the interpreter tunes in, as it were, or understands intuitively the sense of what is being said or chanted, and formulates it in intelligible terms. "The interpretation," writes Laurentin, "may be notably shorter or longer than the speaking in tongues" (*op. cit.*, p. 65). Sometimes the speaker in a tongue speaks an actual language, which someone in the assembly happens to know, and gives the translation. In this case, the translator does not possess the charism of interpretation. For, as Laurentin says, "Interpretation is not translation" (p. 65).

The "tongues" gives one so gifted a means beyond language, which allows one to praise God, to give thim thanks, to express to him one's love, and to sing his marvels in a more profound manner than one is capable of doing with intelligible words. St. Paul says that "we do not know what we should pray for as we ought, but the Spirit pleads for us with unutterable groanings" (Rm 8:26-27). The speaker in tongues becomes aware that "the Spirit in person joins himself to his spirit," as the Apostle says; that the Spirit knocks at the door of his heart and asks him to open it to him. When the speaker of tongues has surrendered himself wholly, the Holy Spirit frees his breath and makes him sing, by giving him a power and an assurance that are not his own. He becomes conscious that this breath wells up from the deepest depths of his being, that the chant is not his, that it is the expression of a love which is not his but of another who dwells in him: the Spirit of the Father and of the Son: the Love of the Three Divine Persons.

While ordinary language is the instrument of communication of one person with another, the speaking in tongues is the expression of life. In "tongues" one uses something better than intelligible language, one uses the breath which is the expression of the depths of life itself. The song in tongues is the breath of love of the Spirit in the one who chants. That is why St. Paul says of the speaker in tongues that "his spirit prays," and that he "prays with the spirit," that is to say, with what is precisely deepest in him; in other words, with his "heart," in the biblical meaning of the word, where the Holy Spirit dwells. The chant in tongues does without conceptual expressions, which are constructed in our head; it instead flows directly and freely from the profound sources of his "heart," vivified by the Spirit. Thus the chant in tongues is truly an "inspired song," as St. Paul says (Ep 5:19); it is a beautiful song which interiorizes and gives peace and joy. Nevertheless, this form of prayer does not mean that we should not also pray with the intelligence. "If I pray in a tongue, my spirit prays," says St. Paul, "but my understanding is unfruitful. What then, is to be done? I will pray with the spirit, but I will pray also with the understanding; I will sing with the spirit, but I will sing with the understanding also" (1 Cor 14:14-15). The whole man must pray: spirit, intelligence and body.

The "gift of tongues" is an incentive to humility. It asks the speaker to make himself very small; to recognize his poverty, since he must talk what sounds as much gibberish, stammer his prayer in unintelligible words, like a child; and to let the Spirit supply strength for his helplessness and ignorance.

The "gift of tongues," by manifesting sensibly the transforming action of the Spirit, increases the speaker's faith and love, as well as his hope, since it makes him understand that he can be transformed in other areas of his being. Consequently, the charism is a sign which calls him to change, it encourages him by freeing him from his fears and anxieties and by showing that the Holy Spirit can change him by his power into a new being.

It is thus that the "gift of tongues" edifies the speaker, and aids him to become a "spiritual man," provided, of course, that he consents to surrender himself wholly to the Spirit, for nothing in the spiritual life is realized automatically and definitively. The efficacy of this gift, like all gifts of God, depend on our constant cooperation.

This charism is given primarily for the spiritual profit of the person on whom it is conferred. That is why it is more profitable that he pray "in tongues" privately, by himself.

However, it can also profit the assembly, when either the speaker himself or another gives an interpretation, and all those present will be edified. In this case, the speaking "in tongues" becomes a sensible and extraordinary manifestation of the Holy Spirit. It is also the sign of his presence and intervention in the group, who can also receive an increase of faith, hope and love. Finally, "tongues are intended as a sign to unbelievers" (1 Cor 14:22).

The Catholic renewal does not necessarily link this charism with the reception of Baptism or of Confirmation. To "speak in tongues" is not the initiatory and obligatory sign of these Sacraments. The sign *par excellence* is the love of God and of neighbor. The significance of the charismatic renewal does not rest on the gift of tongues. This is the least and most humble of all the charisms. Though St. Paul gives thanks to God that he speaks in tongues (1 Cor 14:18); though he wishes that all would talk in tongues like he does; and though he says to them: "Do not hinder the gift of speaking in tongues" (14:39), he prefers that they would rather all prophesy: "For he who prophesies is greater than he who speaks in tongues" (14:5). He has told them earlier: "Strive after the gifts of the Spirit, but especially that you may prophesy" (14:1).

The gift of prophecy is another charism, the existence of which is affirmed not only by St. Paul, but by other writers of the New Testament as well as by those of the Old Testament.

To prophesy is not, first nor principally, to foretell the future. It is, according to the technological meaning of the word, to speak in the name or in the place of God, as I have already pointed out earlier in this book, although the person who prophesies may also foretell future events. The prophet then is one who enlightened by the Holy Spirit, proclaims the message of God, and is a witness of divine realities. In the charismatic renewal, the "prophecy" is most often a word taken from Scripture; it is uttered by a member of the prayer meeting to "edify" the group in their faith, hope and love. St. Paul says that "he who prophesies speaks to men for edification, and encouragement, and consolation" (1 Cor 14:3); that he prophesies so "that all may learn and may be encouraged" (14:31).

The "prophet" hears such and such a word or phrase of Scripture in the interior of himself; he feels strongly urged to utter it, but he is not constrained in such a way that he ceases to be free. If he yields to the inspiration, he utters the word or phrase such as it is, or retouched by him. It is uttered generally in the first person singular with such force, or as the Apostle says, with such "power of the Spirit," that it goes straight to the heart of all, or of one of the group. It affects hearts and consciences as if God or our Lord himself had spoken it.

Sometimes the prophetic message has no direct relation to Scripture, but it is a personal message, admonition or interpolation. In this case, it is necessary to use prudence and to let the "discernment of spirits" intervene, above all when the words assert something predicatively. Prophecies must be judged by the community or by those who preside in the Church, the Bishops, if necessary. Of prophets St. Paul says "let two or three speak at a meeting and let the rest act as judges" (1 Cor 14:30).

I have just mentioned another charism, which St. Paul, St. John and Tradition stress greatly: the discernment of spirits. "Discern what is good," (Rm 12:2). "To another is given the charism of distinguishing of spirits (1 Cor 12:10); "Walk as children of light, testing what is pleasing to God" (Ep 5:9-10); "Beloved, do not believe every spirit, but test the spirits to see whether they are of God" (1 Jn 4:1). Not all who speak in tongues or prophesy do so under the inspiration of the Holy Spirit; hence, comes the recommendation of St. Paul: "Do not extinguish the Spirit. Do not despise prophecies. But test all things; hold fast that which is good. Keep yourselves from every kind of evil" (1 Th 5:21).

There must be a constant care to discern the authenticity of the action of the Spirit. I am going to state clearly and immediately that its exercise involves not only the gift of tongues and that of prophecy but also the whole spiritual life of the Christian. The Apostle says to the Romans: "Be not conformed to this world, but be transformed in the newness of your mind, that you may discern what is the good and acceptable and perfect will of God." That is why, though the charismatic renewal contains elements of an experience that belong particularly to it, such as "speaking in tongues" and "prophecy," it needs no other criterion of discernment than those of the spiritual doctrine of the Church in general.

First of all, what must be understood by "spirits?" Two things: the various inspirations which move us interiorly toward such or such direction, and their source. Now, inspirations can come from ourselves, i.e., from the "new man," which urges us to the good, or from the "old man," which draws us to evil. They can come, secondly, from the "world," here meaning the entirety of man—secularized society—whose spirit and outlook are opposed to the spirit of Christ, the world that is slave to the triple concupiscence St. John speaks of in one of his Letters: "All that is in the world is the lust of the flesh, and the lust of the eyes, and the pride of life; which is not from the Father, but from the world" (1 Jn 2:16). Through its false maxims, evil pleasures and perverse examples, the "world" acts on us to lead us to evil. Thirdly, the inspiriations can come from the evil spirits, who incite or solicit us to evil, or from good spirits, the faithful angels, who lead us to good. Finally, the inspirations have their source from God who through his Spirit, works upon us.

To discern the spirits means then, to learn to distinguish the inspirations which come from a good spirit: the Holy Spirit, the angelic spirits or our spirit aided by grace, from those which come from evil spirits: the fallen angels, the spirit of the "world," and the spirit of our "old man," or the "flesh." It is to judge, whether it involves oneself, another person or a group, if such and such a word or action, decision, attitude, conduct, sentiment and so forth, is inspired by the Spirit of God or by one's own spirit, or by the spirit of evil. In short, we must endeavor to ascertain "the spirit of truth and the spirit of error" (1 Jn 4:6).

To attain this judgment, the Spirit grants a special charism which is a spiritual sense, an understanding renewed by the Spirit, an infused faculty to know and to "feel" and to "savor" what is good. This charism is communicated to some in a particular manner, but all Christians are invited to ask for it and develop it, in order to exercise it for oneself and for others.

The discernment of spirits is done according to certain criteria. One judges the tree for its fruits. Now in the Letter to the Galatians, St. Paul lists a number of fruits of the evil spirits and those of the good spirits:

> *Now the works of the flesh are manifest, which are immorality, uncleanness, licentiousness, idolatry, witchcrafts, enmities, contentions, jealousies, anger, quarrels, factions, parties, envies, murders, drunkenness, carousings, and such like.* (5:19-21).

Then these actions come from the inspiration of the evil spirits. We may add: all that causes troubles, disorders, restlessness, sadness and despair; all which comes from pride, false humility, a hard and closed heart, a false and bitter zeal, from presumption, aggression, obstinacy and so forth. Alas, a person speaks under the inspiration of the evil spirit who says things that are not in harmony with the faith and consequently, with the official doctrines of the Church. He acts under the evil influence who disobeys legitimate authority, and does not conduct himself in conformity with this duty of the state of life.

These are the "fruits of the Spirit: love, joy, peace, patience, kindness, goodness, faith, modesty, continency" (Gal 5:22). We must add: "justice and truth": (Ep 4:9) humility, forgiveness, prudence, trust in God, right intention, unselfishness, simplicity, interior mortification, spiritual liberty, and above all, of course, the love and imitation of Jesus Christ.

I will conclude this discussion of the charisms of "speaking in tongues," and of "prophecy," by saying that if we must give the importance to them that they merit, whose extraordinary and spectacular character astound our rationalist and positivist spirit, we must put them in their proper place in the hierarchy of supernatural values. They come after love.

> *If I should speak with the tongues of men and of angels, but do not have love, I have become as sounding brass or a tinkling cymbal. If I have prophecy and know all mysteries, and if I have all faith so as to remove mountains, yet do not have love, I am nothing. If I distribute all my goods to feed the poor, and if I deliver my body to be burned, yet do not have love it profits me nothing.*

> *Love is patient, is kind; does not envy, is not pretentious, is not puffed up, is not ambitious, is not self-seeking, is not provoked; thinks no evil, does not rejoice over wickedness, but rejoices with the truth; bears with all things, believes all things, hopes all things, endures all things.*

> *Love never fails, whereas prophecies will disappear, and tongues will cease, and knowledge will be destroyed. For we know in part and we prophesy in part; but when that which is perfect has come, that which is imperfect will be done away with . . . So there abide faith, hope and love; these three; but the greatest of these is love* (1 Cor 13:1-13).

Here is what Vatican II had said about charisms in general, before the charismatic renewal spread in the Catholic Church:

> *It is not only through the sacraments of the Church ministries that the same Holy Spirit sanctifies and leads the People of God and enriches it with virtues. Alotting His gifts "to everyone according as he will"* (1 Cor 12:11), *He*

*distributes special graces among the faithful of every rank.
By these gifts He makes them fit and ready to undertake the
various tasks or offices advantageous for the renewal and
upbuilding of the Church, according to the words of the
Apostle: "The manifestation of the Spirit is given to
everyone for profits" (1 Cor 12:7). These charismatic gifts,
whether they be the most outstanding or the more simple and
widely diffused, are to be received with thanksgiving and
consolation, for they are exceedingly suitable and useful for
the needs of the Church. (Lumen Gentium, No. 12).*

The members of the charismatic renewal are aware of these words. It
is with "thanksgiving and consolation" that they wish to receive these
gifts and to exercise them prayerfully without rashness or presumption, but "in the liberty of the Spirit who 'breathes where he wills,' and
in communion with their brothers in Christ, and particularly with
their pastors."

To conclude this chapter, I should not do better than to quote
the words of Pope Paul VI, taken from his Allocution of May 19,
1975, to the participants of the 3rd International Congress of the
Renewal, which took place in Rome:

*The Church and the world have need more than ever that the
wonder of Pentecost continues in history. Indeed, intoxicated by its conquests, modern man has arrived at the
point of imagining himself that, according to the expression
of the last Council "he is an end to himself, the sole artisan
and creator of his own history" (Gaudium et Spes No.
20).Alas! With how many of those very ones who continue,
by tradition, to profess His existence and continue to give
Him a cult, hasn't God become a stranger in their life?
Nothing is more necessary to a world, increasingly
secularized, than the witness of this "spiritual renewal,"
which we see the Holy Spirit raising up today in regions and
milieus the most diverse. . . This "spiritual renewal," couldn't
it be a chance for the Church and for the world? And how, in
this case, can we not use all the means that remain.*